INSIGHTS
ON POLICY ISSUES

VOLUME II

ADDITIONAL BOOKS BY THE AUTHOR

1. Adizes, I. *Industrial Democracy: Yugoslav Style*. New York Free Press, 1971.

2. Adizes, I. and E. Mann-Borgese, eds. *Self-Management: New Dimensions to Democracy*. Santa Barbara, CA: ABC-CLIO, 1975.

3. Adizes, I. *How to Solve the Mismanagement Crisis*. Homewood, IL: Dow Jones/Irwin, 1979.

4. Adizes, I. *Corporate Lifecycles: How and Why Corporations Grow and Die and What to Do About It*. Englewood Cliffs, NJ: Prentice Hall, 1988.

5. Adizes, I. *Mastering Change: The Power of Mutual Trust and Respect in Personal Life, Family Life, Business & Society*. Santa Monica, CA: Adizes Institute, 1991.

6. Adizes, I. *Managing Corporate Lifecycles*: An updated and expanded look at the Corporate Lifecycles. First printing, Paramus, NJ: Prentice Hall Press, 1999. Additional printings by the Adizes Institute Publications.

7. Adizes, I. *Pursuit of Prime*. First printing Santa Monica, CA: Knowledge Exchange, 1996. Additional printings by the Adizes Institute Publications.

8. Adizes, I. *The Ideal Executive: Why You Cannot Be One and What to Do About It*. Santa Barbara, CA: The Adizes Institute Publications, 2004.

9. Adizes, I. *Management/Mismanagement Styles: How to Identify a Style and What to Do About It*. Santa Barbara, CA: The Adizes Institute Publications, 2004.

10. Adizes, I. *Leading the Leaders: How to Enrich Your Style of Management and Handle People Whose Style Is Different from Yours*. Santa Barbara, CA: The Adizes Institute Publications, 2004.

11. Adizes, I. *How to Manage in Times of Crisis (And How to Avoid a Crisis in the First Place)*. Santa Barbara, CA: The Adizes Institute Publications, 2009.

12. Adizes, I. *Insights on Management*. Santa Barbara, CA: The Adizes Institute Publications, 2011.

13. Adizes, I. *Insights on Policy*. Santa Barbara, CA: The Adizes Institute Publications, 2011.

14. Adizes, I. *Insights on Personal Growth*. Santa Barbara, CA: The Adizes Institute Publications, 2011.

15. Adizes, I. *Food for Thought: On Management*. Santa Barbara, CA: The Adizes Institute Publications, 2013.

16. Adizes, I. *Food for Thought: On Change and Leadership*. Santa Barbara, CA: The Adizes Institute Publications, 2013.

17. Adizes, I. *Food for Thought: On What Counts in Life*. Santa Barbara, CA: The Adizes Institute Publications, 2013.

INSIGHTS
ON POLICY ISSUES

VOLUME II

ICHAK KALDERON ADIZES

Founder and CEO, Adizes Institute
Santa Barbara County, California

Library of Congress Cataloging-in-Publication Data

Adizes, Ichak.
Insights on Policy Issues, Volume II

Library of Congress Control Number Pending

ISBN: 978-0-937120-27-9

Published by Adizes Institute Publications
1212 Mark Avenue
Carpinteria, Santa Barbara County, California, USA 93013
805-565-2901; Fax 805-565-0741
Website: www.adizes.com

Design and layout by Dana Levy, Perpetua Press
Printed in the United States of America

Additional copies may be ordered from www.adizes.com/store

To Karim Massimov
Prime Minister of Kazakhstan
With my respects and admiration
for outstanding leadership

CONTENTS

PART III: CHALLENGES FOR THE UNITED STATES

PART IV: ECONOMIC AND LEGAL CHALLENGES

Part V: Global Challenges in Leading Change

Part VI: Social Challenges

INTRODUCTION

A BLOG HAS MANY SOURCES and many reasons for being, but usually only one voice. And that voice makes it distinctive. Reading over many of the blogs reprinted in this book, I see that my voice is sometimes contrarian and controversial, sometimes that of a curmudgeon, and at other times to my surprise the cry of a passionate populist. It is almost always informed by my experiences and travels in foreign lands—most recently in Russia, Ukraine, Greece and Israel.

My travels are of course not those of a tourist intent on sightseeing. I am the CEO of the Adizes Institute, which is both a training academy for international managers and corporate consultants and—its main function—an international management consultant firm. When I travel—and I am in a foreign land about 80% of the year—I am meeting with clients, corporations and their leaders, and also from time to time with national political leaders and heads of government. They are all sources for much of my information and the centerpieces for most of my observations. Without them there would be few insights and no blogs.

But of course I am also curious. Curious to see life in the restaurants and coffee shops and streets filled with people who live in these foreign countries. And here my facility with languages is an enormous help.

In Russia I have met with banking executives and government officials from all of the Russian states. Our aim is clear-cut: to explore ways of making the economy more effective and efficient...and not incidentally, to find ways to infuse mutual trust and respect into the nation's economic structure. In Greece my meetings were with corporate and political leaders to examine once again the quagmire into which that nation was sinking. Visits to Israel are always a form of returning home, although I have lived in the United States since 1963, but also of conferring with leaders. Readers of my weekly blog may find occasional changes in these pages. They reflect in some measure a rethinking on my part, a response to points raised by letters from readers who are, I am pleased to say, quite vocal. Or I simply may be reacting to a historical shift within the policies and politics of the world in which we live.

Some of these observations may appear outdated, even out of touch. I decided nevertheless to include them in this Volume II of my insights because I believe they have value: If nothing else they suggest how the world was perceived at the time. And in fact some of my insights have proved to be right, predicting what actually happened later on.

A final word about the weekly blogs for new readers. They are posted every Friday on my website (www.ichakadizes.com/blog) and are sent by e-mail to thousands of subscribers. It is free. I began them in 2003.

It should be noted these are insights, more akin to perceptions than conclusions based on research and scholarship. As always, they are placed "out there" for your comments and criticism. I see it is as my continuing dialogue with the world.

Without fear of criticism. Without pretention to be right either.

Ichak Kalderon Adizes, Ph.D.

PART I

✦

COUNTRIES IN TRANSITION

DIAGNOSIS: THE DRUG CARTELS OF MEXICO[1]

I VISIT MEXICO MONTHLY on various consulting assignments. This essay is based on conversations I have had recently with leading Mexicans; it represents my diagnosis of issues relating to the drug trade there.

A $32 billion business

The Mexican drug trade is conservatively estimated to be a $32 billion business. That's more than big enough to buy off not only the countless mules who carry the drugs into the United States, but also enough to buy off corrupt police officers and politicians.

The cartels are fighting a bloody war for dominance.

Here's another unpleasant reality: The cartels are fighting a bloody war for dominance. Each time the Mexican government catches a leader of one of the cartels it ignites a new round of inter-gang bloodshed. Most of the murders are cartel members killing one another or the mules of a competing cartel. Some of the dead are policemen who did not heed warnings to stay out of the conflicts.

As if that weren't enough, the crime rate in Mexico is growing. Kidnapping for ransom is on the rise; the victims are typically businessmen and well-to-do professionals like doctors.

One more stark fact to consider: The US has established free trade in armaments. This enables the cartels to buy machine guns and other lethal weapons easily, and then transfer them to Mexico.

The kidnappings for ransom are most probably not related to the drug trade. Mexico has had kidnappings for ransom for as long as anyone can remember. The problem might be more acute now, however, because the police have

1. Adizes Insights, November 2010.

been compromised by the drug cartels and are comparatively ineffective. This is Mexico's problem.

The same cannot be said of the drug problem, because only a very small percentage of the illegal drugs are intended for the local Mexican market. Most of them are destined for the US. Mexico is not even the main producer of the drugs that cross its borders; it is mostly a distribution center.

What is happening, as I see it, is that the US has the problem, but is putting the burden to solve it on the Mexicans.

For years, America has "exported" its wars to foreign lands: Fight the radical Muslims in Afghanistan or Iraq, so they do not advance to the US. This has happened before, too. Fighting in Korea and Vietnam was meant to halt Communist expansion, and fighting in Europe had the goal of stopping Nazi expansion.

The problem is that drugs remain a big business.

The difference now is that Americans aren't doing the fighting. Instead of America aggressively fighting the cartels, it is asking the Mexican government to do the job. At the same time, for purely political reasons, it is not delegitimizing the sale of arms that end up in Mexico and fuel the inter-cartel wars.

The problem is that drugs remain a big business. The way to solve the problem is to "drain the swamp where the mosquitoes dwell" by destroying the business. That is what former president of Mexico Vicente Fox is trying to accomplish by advocating the legalization of drugs.

In my opinion, though, this legitimization of the drug trade will not solve the problem. It will only make narcotics a legal business, which means legal entities will develop distribution centers, advertise, and make the problem even worse.

To totally destroy the business, Ricardo Salinas Pliego suggests that hospitals dispense these drugs for free, as we are currently doing with condoms and needles to stop AIDS from spreading. He also advocates that we launch big campaigns to educate people about the dangers of drugs, and that we set up a network of free clinics to treat drug addicts.

It's a good idea. If this were done, there would be no drug business. The honey would disappear, which means the flies would disappear, too.

There is a catch, however. These measures must be undertaken in the US. If Mexico did all of this on their side of the border it would not solve the problem, because the real business is being done in the US, not in Mexico.

If I advised the Mexican government, I would say, "Leave the drug cartels alone. This is America's problem, not yours. Your focus should be on your problem, which is the kidnappings. Communicate to the drug cartels that they must peacefully divide their territories and stop their wars and help the government stop the kidnappings, in exchange for the Mexican government looking the other way."

What about the Americans? I would advise them to listen to what Salinas Pliego says. There is merit in his suggestion. Drugs are not a legal problem but a health and education problem. Prosecuting drug addicts does not stop the use of drugs. Drug addicts are sick. Subjecting them to legal penalties only makes the price of drugs go up, which means the addicts need to be more courageous to be able to afford them. That means the profitability of the distributors becomes even bigger, and it also means that bigger, stronger, and more ruthless dealers are attracted to the business.

The criminalization of drug use only makes the drug trade stronger, not weaker.

Will the US ever follow this advice? I doubt it.

In the meantime, Mexicans are dying.

A Culture of Fear[1]

I N PREVIOUS BLOG POSTS I have reported that one the characteristics of the Russian managerial culture is fear.

Take Mr. X, head of department Y. When department Y meets, he is the only one to talk. The rest listen and, if they participate, they would never say anything that could be interpreted as criticizing authority. But when Mr. X attends the meeting of his boss, now he is totally quiet like his subordinates were quiet in his department meeting.

> *It is as if the head is detached from the body.*

The repercussions of this behavior are that there is low flow of information from the bottom up. It is as if the head is detached from the body. The head imagines what is going on but he or she does not really know for sure and no amount of management by walking around helps.

(I am trying hard to break this culture by instituting Adizes hard rules. As I control the dominance of the meeting that Mr. X exhibits and create a safe environment for others to talk, I am starting to see results: People are starting to talk more freely.)

But I have noticed another phenomenon.

On May 1, over 100,000 people marched in Moscow's Red Square celebrating the day of the worker. They marched with slogans such as "Stop corruption," "For a better living salary," "In unity is our strength," etc. People were holding balloons and flowers, and for the first time in Russia I saw accordion players in the crowd. It was very celebratory.

I walked up and down the march for over two hours. Not once did I get a person to smile at me, or make eye contact. Not one person said hello to

1. Adizes Insights, May 2012.

me. I did ask people questions. I got a short answer and they moved on. They could have asked where am I from, anything. But there was no contact. It is not that they were busy marching. They were standing for more than an hour waiting for the march to start.

But this phenomenon is not exclusive to the march. People do not smile. A bank teller told me that she decided to smile, to be friendly, to be different. People felt threatened by her behavior. They even told her so. She was different and thus rejected.

What is normal is not a question of ethics. It is one of statistics. If the mode of behavior is not to smile, that is normal. And the one who smiles is abnormal.

I asked the bank teller what she thought the reason was for not smiling, not making eye contact.

"Because when you smile the other person will wonder what is it you want from him or her. They will feel you are trying to manipulate them. That you want something from them and they resent it."

An accordion player in Moscow

I reported in a previous blog post that I have looked and looked, asked and asked, where I could find accordion playing in Moscow. A small accordion with buttons on both sides is the national instrument. Look at Russian paintings of celebrations and you will see an accordion being played.

There were over twenty accordion players I counted in the march. They played well. But nowhere in Moscow can you find a restaurant or coffee shop with live accordion music. Many restaurants in Belgrade have live music and the guests sing as food is served. The same is true in Mexico, Greece, and Israel. Even in the US one can find piano bars where people stand around the piano player and sing melodies from musicals. But not in Russia.

"Don't you ever get together and sing?" I asked.

"Oh, we do sing in the kitchen," a secretary told me, "or at a wedding, but otherwise no."

There is singing in karaoke bars, and there are lots of those bars around. But spontaneous singing not directed by a screen—no, there is none.

What is going on, I wondered. Russia has a romantic culture. I know of no other country where there are flower shops every two hundred yards, open twenty-four hours a day, seven days a week. I know of no other country where they worship their poets like they do in Russia. The sculptures of

Pushkin and Mayakovski are everywhere. Plaques are posted on houses informing passersby that a certain musician, composer, painter, poet, or author lived and created there during such and such years.

Moscow has lots of cultural life. Classical music is performed in multiple locations almost every night. Theater is thriving. Ballet. Opera. Lots of restaurants. Still there is no spirit. No soul. I cannot explain it. It has to be experienced. It is something you feel when you land in, say, Rio de Janeiro during Carnival. It is something you feel when you enter a Mexican restaurant with mariachis playing.

The Communist system killed the spirit of Russians.

I was in Guadalajara for the Mariachi Festival. The opera house where the festival was held had over a thousand people. More than once the audience joined the mariachis on the stage with singing. I felt the roof was going to come off.

Two days ago I attended a celebration of Russian national dances in Moscow. National folk dancing groups were singing and dancing the folk dances of the various regions of Russia. No one ever joined the musicians and singers on the stage with singing. The audience watched, clapped their hands, and that was it.

The aftermath of Communism

I do not believe this is the genuine Russian culture. Read their literature describing life in the pre-Communist era. They were dancing and singing then. So what is going on? Why no community singing? Why no smiling?

My explanation is that the Communist system killed the spirit of Russians. It destroyed their communal soul. It destroyed family unity. Monogamous behavior was considered to be "very bourgeoisie."

Communism instilled fear. Fear of strangers. Fear of differences. Fear of authority.

It is the Communist regime, with its rule of fear, that took the soul out of the Russian culture. The Communist regime made brothers spy on each other and report suspicious political behavior to the secret police. It educated children to spy on their parents, and if a parent expressed any criticism of the regime, to report it immediately to the police.

Communism instilled fear and lack of trust in anybody and anything. Husbands could not trust their wives. Parents could not trust their children.

By breaking trust, Communism created a culture where one has to be on the watch all the time, not knowing where the next threat to your existence will come from. It may come from a smiling person.

Communism was defeated forty years ago, but the culture of fear still lingers. Communism was, I think, like the Chernobyl disaster. It will take some generations for the toxic environment to change and soulful life come back to Russia.

AN OPEN LETTER TO MR. MEDVEDEV[1]
(Prime Minister, the Russian Federation)

June 23, 2012

Dear Mr. Medvedev,

The media informs us repeatedly of your commitment to increasing entrepreneurship and innovation in Russia. The purpose of this letter is to provide an analysis of what needs to be done in order for that to happen.

Entrepreneurship and innovation require psychological energy of the entrepreneur or innovator because "to entrepreneur" means to do something new, and in starting something new there is always uncertainty and risk. Both consume psychological energy.

Uncertainty consumes energy because the innovator has to imagine what has to be done and how. The information is not given. It has to be created, and creativity consumes energy.

Uncertainty and risk

Uncertainty can be high in a country in transition or still developing. There are no competent marketing research entities, no reliable governmental statistical reporting agencies, no easily accessible information about how to, for instance, get a license or a permit, etc.

Now, how about risk? Risk consumes psychological energy because the entrepreneurial endeavor might not succeed; the investment of time and money might be lost. Worries consume lots of energy.

Imagine a situation in which the government is not only big and bureaucratic, but also corrupt. There is a chance that if your business succeeds, corrupt government officials might take it from you by fabricating accusa-

1. Adizes Insights, July 2012.

tions against you. Or perhaps they will award licenses and moneymaking opportunities to a competitor who is either paying bribe money or is owned indirectly by those in power. In this unfair competition, your risk might be prohibitive.

Here is a Russian example: A Russian businessman whose company imported medical equipment was negotiating a $200 million deal with a Dutch company. One day during the negotiations, the police showed up at his home, handcuffed him, and put him in jail. They produced no search warrant and no reason for their action, and refused him access to an attorney. After three months, the police visited him in jail and told him he was free to go home. Again, no explanation was given, either for why he was jailed or why he was being released.

Would you invest in a country like that? Would you start a business in a country like that?

When he returned to work, he discovered that his competition had made a deal with the Dutch company he had been negotiating with. He believes that the competition simply isolated him by bribing the police to arrest him. Then, they stole his deal.

Sure, he can sue. But whom? How? The court, he believes, is corrupt too. Everyone appears to be for sale.

Would you invest in a country like that? Would you start a business in a country like that?

If entrepreneurs have any choice, they will put their money in a place where the risk is controllable and the uncertainty manageable. Those who do not have a choice keep a low profile; thus, entrepreneurship is stymied, and so is innovation. Why take the risk? Why endure sleepless nights?

I acknowledge that foreign investment capital continues, so far, to come in to Russia. Does this fact contradict my analysis?

I suggest that these are investments with a short payback period. These investors want to get their money out as soon as possible. They do not stay and develop the country. On the contrary, in order to manage their risk they exploit the country as much and as quickly as possible. Naturally.

But this is not what you are looking for. From my understanding from the media, you are trying to increase local, indigenous, Russian innovation and entrepreneurship.

In order to encourage entrepreneurship, the government needs to reduce uncertainty and reduce risk.

To reduce uncertainty the government should be working hard on debureaucratization of its processes, and provide information that is reliable and consistent.

And to reduce risk it must stop corruption, first and above all.

It is either corruption or entrepreneurship. It cannot be both.

Management education for increased entrepreneurship and high-tech centers for innovation might project to the public that the government is taking action, but that is not where the root problem is and thus not where the root solution can be found.

Thank you, Mr. Prime Minister.

Sincerely,
Prof. Dr. Ichak Kalderon Adizes
President, the Adizes Institute
Santa Barbara, California, USA

Quo Vadis, Russia?[1]

I HAVE BEEN ON A PANEL with Prime Minister of the Russian Federation Dmitry Medvedev at the Investors Forum in Sochi on September 20, 2012. At the forum I was asked an important question by the moderator, which, due to time constraints I could not fully answer. I take this opportunity to answer it in writing.

The question was: "In your opinion, Dr. Adizes, what are the causes of the fear that Russian managers exhibit in their management practice?"

There are two major reasons for the fear.

Spying on parents

The first reason: You have probably heard about people whose legs have been amputated but who continue to feel pain in their limbs even after they were gone. Some people with this condition also experience tingling, cramps, burning, and freezing. Apparently, memories are stronger than reality.

In the Jewish book of the elders, Divrey Avot, it says that in a house where a person hanged to death it is forbidden to talk about ropes. Why? Like a phantom limb, words can evoke past experiences that, in turn, arouse strong emotions—emotions that are unrelated to those words' present context.

Using these analogies, let me broach a subject that is rarely discussed: the tragic accident in Russia's history that has fundamentally impacted the behavior of its people. I am referring to the Stalinist era, when brothers were ordered to spy on brothers, husbands to spy on their wives, and wives to spy on their husbands. Small children were even encouraged to spy on their parents.

I remember in Yugoslavia when I was ten years old—a "Young Pioneer"

1. Adizes Insights, September 2012.

with a red scarf around my neck—I was told by my team leader that my real father was Tito, and that if I heard my parents saying anything against Tito, I was to immediately report them to the police. This was not a Yugoslav invention. It was imported from the Soviet Union.

What impact do you think this history has on Russia today? Suspicion. Fear. Russia as a nation has lived through a serious trauma and is still suffering from it. It is called "post-traumatic stress disorder."

Let me give you two examples to illustrate.

A story about East Germany

When diagnosing problems in Russia, even today, people quickly start asking themselves: "Who should be blamed? Who is at fault?" It takes them practically no time to move from what is wrong to who is wrong. The process can easily deteriorate into a dangerous witch-hunt.

Here is a true story of how fear dominates social consciousness. It happened to one of my Institute Associates recently in East Germany. The unification of Germany happened twenty years ago. The fear that was the hallmark of the Communist era should have dissipated. But in the national consciousness, fear is not so easy to purge.

A group of managers was seated in a half-circle. My associate suggested, as a warm-up exercise, that each participant tell the group something about themselves that no one knew. In the West, this warm-up exercise is practiced frequently, and the participants tend to talk about hobbies or trips they have taken. Very innocent. But that day in East Germany there was complete silence. No one volunteered to say anything.

During the break, the Adizes Associate asked one of the participants why no one had spoken. The participant looked at him, his eyes cold, and said: "And how do you intend to use this information?"

Do you hear the fear?

How should the fear be treated? By reliving it. The more you try to put it out of your mind, the more you try to forget it, the longer it stays with you.

A way to free Russia from its past

Across from the Marriott Aurora hotel in Moscow there is the Gulag History Museum. It seems that it is supported by private donations exclusively. I am very sorry to tell you it is the most run-down, dilapidated museum I have ever seen.

This is a mistake.

If Russia's leaders want to free this nation from the relentless fear implanted in its consciousness by the atrocities of the Stalin era, they should build the best, largest museum possible and accurately document the disaster Stalin perpetrated on Russia. Make it mandatory that children visit the museum, that no one graduates from school without taking a course about the atrocities of that era.

If the country is enabled to face the trauma directly, the fear will diminish. That is what is necessary if you want to increase innovation and entrepreneurship, because neither can flourish in an atmosphere of fear.

Deluged by new laws

There is a second reason for the fear, may I suggest, and it is the following: When a country experiences major transitions, as Russia has, it often legislates a lot of new laws and regulations, right on top of the old ones. Take accounting systems: I am told that there are four different accounting systems in Russia. Which one is the right one to use?

Businessmen simply cannot keep track of all the new laws, particularly the ones that overlap with old laws. It becomes difficult, if not impossible, to know what is right and legal and what is not. No businessman can avoid violating some rule, usually without knowing it. What they do know is that they are surely guilty of something, and if the government chooses to prosecute (for whatever reason) it can always come up with a violation. The businessman could wind up in jail.

How do entrepreneurs in Russia deal with this risky uncertainty? They have several choices: move out of the country; stay in the country but move their family and all their assets out of the country and have an up-to-date passport with a valid visa, so they can leave the country on short notice; or be well connected with those in power in order to be protected.

What most people can afford to do is none of the above alternatives. They live in constant fear.

Cleaning up the mess

What to do? If I were prime minister, I would appoint a senior first deputy prime minister, the highest in rank after prime minister. I would give him or her a very well-financed ministry to analyze all laws, procedures, and regulations in all the ministries and regional governments, find the overlapping or outdated laws and the regulations that do not make sense, etc., and clean up the mess.

When it becomes clear what businessmen are supposed to be responsible for and what they are not, the fear will diminish.

But this process will do much more. It will also significantly reduce corruption. A messy bureaucracy practically invites corruption by creating the opportunity for corrupt people to demand money for making the system work.

Right now, Russia is fighting corruption by prosecuting the guilty. But that is like killing mosquitoes. Instead of killing the mosquitoes, drain the swamp where they breed.

MANAGERIAL PROBLEMS OF RUSSIA[1]

THIS PAPER IS BASED ON TWO AND A HALF YEARS of experience being exposed to Russian management through lecturing, consulting, and conversing. It does not claim to be scientifically proven; it could be biased. The data source is limited.

Twelve problems

I have identified twelve characteristics of Russian managerial practices that impact the Russian managerial effectiveness.

1. Lack of systematization

It starts with the amorphic language structure. There are multiple ways, all legitimate, to structure a sentence like "I love you." You can say: *I love you, you love I, you I love, love I you*, and *love you I*. They all mean the same. There is no single way to structure it right. If one watches how Russians drive, it is the same as how they structure a sentence: Anything goes. No rules are really adhered to. In Adizes language, this is lack of (A) reflected in no discipline.

2. Lack of discipline

Watch how people drive. How they park. How they handle their garbage. There is no discipline. It is as if people do not take rules seriously unless there is a serious repercussion to their deviation from the rule. As a result, managers have to overuse power to get discipline. Serious punishments. Levying heavy penalties. Mild ones do not work. It seems as if the population has been so heavily punished that they are immune to mild punishments. (The more power that has been used, the more that will have to be used to get the same results; on the margin, power has a declining effectiveness.)

1. Adizes Insights, November 2013. Accepted for publication by *Harvard Business Review*, Russia.

3. Autocratic management

The need to punish in order to get discipline is fed by another characteristic of Russian management, one which is not necessarily a remnant of Communism but of the general history of Russia: authoritarianism. A manager or leader seeks out and will fight whomever challenges their authority. There is an air of superiority that any leader in a Russian organization has to demonstrate. He cannot admit to being fallible. A leader, by admitting to not knowing it all, fears he might lose authority because it is expected that he knows it all.

> *One of the characteristics of the Russian managerial culture is fear.*

4. Control orientation

Autocracy leads to the need to control. The way one region is organized has to be the way all regions should be organized. The purpose is to get as much sameness as possible. That increases the capacity to control what is going on. But this orientation impacts performance. For performance, one has to pay attention to the peculiarities of each geography, each market. Sameness impacts performance adversely. It is another cause of ineffectiveness.

5. Moscow centricity

The autocratic style and the need to control are not only personalized. It is institutionalized where decisions are being made. Moscow is the center of the Russian universe. Moscow decides often without listening to what the rest of Russia needs or has to say. I am not referring just to government. This is also true for corporations.

6. Fear

Autocracy and control breed fear and one of the characteristics of the Russian managerial culture is fear. People are afraid to challenge, to speak up. It is wiser to lie down and be compliant; not to get into trouble. In Russia when the top person shows up in a meeting, there is fear that if one challenges the leader in public it will be considered insubordination, which can be dangerous for the survivability of the person expressing himself.

7. Ineffective efficiency

The Soviet Union was not market and profit oriented but efficiency oriented. The assumption was that sameness, control, and autocracy increase efficiency. Thus, the sameness and centralization of services and authority. The assumption apparently was that it creates economies of scale. With the fall of the

Soviet Union, market forces were introduced and over-control and sameness impeded the flexibility needed in a market economy. The result was that the system produced ineffectiveness.

8. *How* rather than *why*

This legacy of focusing on efficiency had its ramifications in organizing a company or in the decision-making process. An inordinate percentage of energy is dedicated to answering the question of *how*, rather than examining *why* we do what we do. Again, the driving force is efficiency rather than effectiveness.

9. Waste

Excessive efficiency orientation has its costs. One of them is diseconomy of scale. On the margin control costs more than it contributes value. On the margin excessive efficiency produces inefficiency.

10. Corruption

The overkill on efficiency creates bureaucracy, which has its negative repercussions, reflected not only in waste. It gives corrupt people the possibility to be corrupt. They are either the ones who know how to maneuver the system so that it can deliver what it exists for, or they are the ones who provide the permits. They can then require extra payment for their service or for abusing their power.

11. Organizations organized around people

The Soviet Union did not just discourage economic entrepreneurship, it even jailed entrepreneurs. They were considered *spekulants*. The end result is that people who are entrepreneurial and can lead are missing. It created a whole class of bureaucrats. The shortage of people with business acumen is causing many organizations to get organized around the people they have or can find and not around tasks the company needs to be performed.

12. Searching for whom to blame

Ineffective bureaucracy and corruption can yield the wrong diagnosis of problems. It is interesting to note how problems get diagnosed. The discussion moves fast from why a problem exists to who is to blame for the problem.

A cultural (not a people) problem

Is there hope? I would say yes. Individually, Russian executives are bright, intelligent, even cunning, and very creative when allowed to be; they are extremely capable individuals.

The problem is not with people but with the culture created by a history of autocracy. And culture can be changed. It only needs committed leadership on a micro, mezzo, or macro level.

Reflections on Travels to Cuba, Ukraine, Serbia, Macedonia, Turkey, Montenegro, and Kazakhstan[1]

I HAVE JUST RETURNED from a visit to all the above countries for work, consulting and lecturing, with one exception: Cuba. That trip was a present from my wife for my seventy-sixth birthday. But I came away from Cuba with observations and perceptions that I want to share with you. To say that the trip, all of it, was a learning experience for me would be an understatement.

Cuba

This country has incredible opportunities for investment. The island has a long coastline (it is an island, after all) and is sparsely populated. There is a great deal of land on which to build new factories, high-tech enterprises, and resorts. The Bahamas fear the time when US sanctions are lifted. They will then have to face enormous competition from Cuba.

> *The Cuban people are well educated, but poorly paid.*

The reasons that underlie the fantastic opportunities for investment are quite clear. The Cuban people are well educated, but poorly paid. They are industrious by nature. There is no corruption to speak of. And its geographic location, a one-hour flight from Miami, is like a gift from God.

As we were driving along the coast of Havana I saw dilapidated looking buildings. It was startling given the magical views. How can this be, I exclaimed. It felt like I was driving along Copacabana in Brazil, where the real estate prices are in the millions.

Under Fidel Castro, the government nationalized all property. It was rented back to families, yes, but only the rooms in the building. The actual building itself is still owned and supposedly managed by the government. The result

1. Adizes Insights, November 2013.

is that inside the building the apartments are well taken care of, while the facade, the entryway, and the stairs are all in total disrepair. What an opportunity to buy the buildings and renovate them. The reality is that it is possible to do just that now. The government is willing to sell.

I said earlier that the Cubans are industrious. You can see that at every street corner. They dress in local-color clothing just so tourists can take pictures with them, for a fee. They sell postcards. Paintings. Anything and everything.

Restaurants sprouted like mushrooms after the rain.

It was forbidden in the past to engage in private enterprise, but the government has relaxed this limitation. Today anyone who wants can open a restaurant...in her home. And what has happened? Restaurants sprouted like mushrooms after the rain. Wherever you look there is a restaurant in the garden, in the living room. But you are not allowed to open a second restaurant. No chains. In other words, it is just the beginning of capitalism. But it is coming.

I believe the US is making a major mistake in holding onto the economic blockade of Cuba. Anyone with a foreign passport can invest in Cuba. Except those with American passports. Not that the Cubans forbid it; the US government forbids it.

So what is happening? Entrepreneurs from everywhere are rushing in. They see the great opportunity, the virgin territory in front of them. The Israelis are there with a major commercial real estate development plan. Investors from other nations are buying up prime real estate and developing their own businesses in Cuba. Only the US is left behind, missing a great window of opportunity. And it's all in plain view, just ninety miles away.

We visited a factory where premier Cuban cigars are made. It was a typical sweatshop factory. People were sitting at rows of tables rolling cigars. There is a quota spelling out how many cigars they need to produce each day. It's a very boring job. Repetitive. Manual. How do they keep the workers interested?

Here I found a very original solution. The factory has a reader. He or she reads the workers novels, poems, and stories as they roll those cigars. These are not just any kind of stories. They are the classics. When we were there a woman was reading *The Count of Monte Cristo*. I was told those workers knew most of the classical literature quite well, no matter how many years of school they had completed. Working in the factory for years, day in and day out, with someone reading them a wonderful book—there is a lot of education going on.

The factory is owned by the government, but it is run like any other for-profit enterprise.

Whoever has the opportunity to visit Cuba, I urge you, go now. The place is changing rapidly and you might miss the opportunity of your life. It is not every day that we can see a country bypassing many of the problems countries in transition from Communism are suffering: corruption, economic stagnation, and dissatisfaction on the part of the people. In general, these problems are not present here. In Cuba I do not see the apathetic look on people's face that I encounter in most countries in transition.

In those other countries trying to manage change there is often a sense of despair. You can see it in the streets, in the shops. In the slope of shoulders that look beaten. Apathy. Loss of hope. You know that corruption is rampant. In Ukraine, Serbia, Bosnia, Russia, those who are able to leave emigrate. The best minds. The result is that those nations face a shortage of managerial resources and the economy suffers. Not in Cuba. I have not seen as many smiling faces in other countries as I saw in Cuba. People are pleasant; they try to please. Not as many are desperate to leave anymore.

Don't misunderstand—the population is very poor. Poorer than the people in Serbia, for example. So why the smiles? Because in Serbia there is frustration with the government. In Cuba the trust link has not been severed. The Cuban government is not corrupt. The political leaders have a vision and an ideology. In reality they have taken many wrong turns and created an economic disaster. However, on paper they look like their intentions are pure and in the people's interest. So, ironically, the populace suffers less.

As long as people feel safe from their government, even if they are poor, they still have energy and a willingness to smile. When the government abuses them, it is like losing trust in your own parents; the smiles quickly are wiped from people's faces. Apathy, pain, and surrendering to one's economic condition prevail. Unless of course one can escape the country.

Turkey

Turkey is blooming if not booming. You can feel it in the supermarkets, in the way the people rush to work, in the bumper-to-bumper traffic, in the construction of new buildings everywhere.

You can feel it in the new, incredibly modern airport, in the business lounge that rivals the one in Dubai in its opulence, and in the generosity with which food is offered. Turkish Airlines justifiably was named the best European airline for the year 2012. Its business class equals the service and comfort of first class on, say, Lufthansa.

Turkey is blooming if not booming. The debate in the Turkish newspapers is all about Prime Minister Recep Tayyip Erdogan's initiative to forbid cohabitation of males and females in the same building at universities. The press is agog: Will his demand be accepted or not?

The whole subject is bogus. There are no cohabited buildings at universities. So what is the debate all about? People believe he is testing the waters to prohibit coeducation all together.

Prime Minister Erdogan is working diligently, it seems to me, to make Turkey a modern Islamic state. Not necessarily run by Sharia, but following Islamic behavioral rules based on Islamic values of modesty; and maintaining the role of women as homemakers who stay at home and take care of the family, instead of becoming career women.

Turkey is thus going through a transition: It is moving from being exclusively a secular state where religion is under the control of secular forces to one where religious values prevail within the state.

Ukraine

It hurts to listen to people describe what is going on here in Ukraine. Corruption is out in the open. The government does not even bother to hide its practices or outcomes.

Here is what some bankers told me: An Italian bank bought a local bank for over a billion dollars. They invested another billion, and gave loans to corporations, but cannot collect those loans because the court system is corrupt. Disgusted, the Italians are selling the bank at five cents on the dollar. Almost a two-billion-dollar loss. And who is buying the bank? A member of the Ukrainian president's family.

Another story: Government deposits money in a bank. The bank gives loans to companies owned by government officials. The companies refuse to pay back the loans. The bank goes bankrupt. Government money ends up in those companies free and clear.

How do you like that?

Anyone who can is trying to get his or her assets out of the country. Whoever can leave tries to find a way out.

Serbia

It is most unfortunate that the country of my birth is actually going bankrupt. I read in the newspapers that the government is planning to lease Vojvodina, a part of the country that has very productive agriculture, to the Arab Gulf states. The country needs money so leasing a whole region is one way to generate funds. It would be equivalent to the US leasing Mississippi.

Obviously the people of Vojvodina are not too happy about this development. Add to it that Vojvodina is populated by people who speak Hungarian because the region borders on Hungary and historically it was part of the Austro-Hungarian Empire. I would not be surprised if the people of Vojvodina start requesting separation from Serbia, much like Kosovo did in the 1990s. If Serbia is not committed to Vojvodina, why should Vojvodina be committed to Serbia?

Another part of Serbia, the Sandjak, populated by Muslims, is making its own noises. It wants more autonomy. This could be a prelude to separation too. The end result is that Serbia might end up being mainly one large city-state called Belgrade.

If I am asked how Serbia fell to its knees, what led to its downfall, my answer is that the cause, rampant corruption, sadly, dates back to Kosovo. It takes an enormous amount of governmental energy to deal with this separation. Initially it required great financial resources to keep Kosovo as part of Serbia. But the government was insistent on supporting Kosovo, and, of course, holding onto it. In 1991 I called Kosovo the Serbian gangrene and urged Serbia's prime minister to let it go its separate, ethnic way. The sooner Serbia cuts it off from the main body of the state, I argued, the quicker Serbia will be able to redirect its energies and solve its own problems.

Today Serbia seems ready to surrender a great deal, including many national heritage symbols. The government is in the process of negotiating to sell its sports teams, Crvena Zvezda (the Red Star) and Partisan, to the Arabs. (Imagine the US selling the Giants or the Patriots to the Chinese.) True it has been done before. Chelsea FC, the English soccer team, was sold to a Russian oligarch. The world is becoming multi-national in more ways than one.

Macedonia

I had not visited Macedonia in five years. After having a public disagreement with the prime minister over a dispute with Greece (I had been consulting with both countries) I decided to keep away from Macedonia. Until things cooled down, I told myself.

What a surprise awaited me.

Billions of dollars, taken as a loan, have been invested in renewing the city of Skopje, the capital. That means art in the form of sculpture every few yards; buildings in baroque style all over the center of the city; large, wide boulevards crisscross the main avenues. No traffic. Taxis are abundant and for two euros one can actually go from one end of the city to another. No reason to drive on your own.

I was impressed with the fiscal policies. The taxes are low: 10% on dividends, and, if profits are reinvested, zero taxes. Personal tax on salaries is 15%, but only on those with a certain upper income. Those with lower salaries pay no taxes whatsoever.

Every store must take your money via a credit card. Or, if you pay in cash, must provide a receipt. If stores are caught not giving a receipt, the penalties are prohibitive: one month's average salary for the first offense; double or triple that for the second offense; and the store is closed for a period of time for a third offense.

The government is harsh and vindictive when it comes to criticism. No one dares to circumvent the tax system. The penalties are high whereas compliance is not too expensive. The result is that there is no gray economy, i.e., people do not avoid paying their taxes (which is not the case in Greece). Tax collection is not an issue.

But the results of this fiscal policy are much more profound than that. Since there is no corruption, and there is law and order, the population feels quite safe and content. The economy is growing. People are satisfied, voting predominantly for the ruling party. In a safe environment, investments pour in from abroad. Macedonia is the most advanced country in the region.

The only complaint I heard is that freedom of speech is limited. The government is harsh and vindictive when it comes to criticism.

I felt that this perceived problem is not a problem at this point in time. To make a transition like this a country needs a strong hand, a hand which is not corrupt and which has a vision. And that hand is the government of Nikola Gruevski.

The problem is that "a strong hand," while functional during the transition today, often resists giving up power tomorrow. The result? It becomes dysfunctional. As to Macedonia, we will see.

The interesting point for me was the issue of an earlier name dispute with Greece. In years past when consulting for the prime minister, I pressed the government to compromise with Greece on the name Macedonia (which the Greeks resented, claiming the name was part of their history and heritage). If Macedonia would agree to a name change, Greece would remove its opposition to Macedonia's to admission to NATO and to the European Union.

I thought that it was imperative for Macedonia to join the EU because of its Albanian minority. This minority kept to itself. It had its educational institutions in the Albanian language from nursery school to the university level. And it had its own enterprises, which were not co-owned with Macedonians. Moreover, they were located in Western Macedonia, where most native Macedonians do not live or visit. It was like a state within a state.

My concern in the past was that if and when Albania joined the EU, or even started negotiations to join, the Macedonian Albanian minority might request separation from Macedonia and seek to affiliate itself with Albania to which they, by language and ethnic affiliation, belong. I thought they would prefer to be in the EU rather than be in an isolated Macedonia.

This is not the case anymore, as I observed in this last visit.

It seems clear (and remarkable) that today Macedonia is doing well. Everywhere you look big cranes are at work constructing high-rise buildings. People look content. And the tax rules are not enforced on the Albanian population, which might have led to friction. Albanians living in Macedonia can still engage in commerce in cash and avoid paying taxes. Moreover, if they want to, they probably can get a second passport from Albania. Many Macedonians (about 40,000 I was told) did just that by taking out a second citizenship in neighboring Bulgaria. By doing so these Macedonians are now members of the EU.

Thus, the Albanian minority population can have their cake and eat it: the benefits of Macedonia as well as the benefits of Albania and, indirectly, of the EU. The pressure on Macedonia to join the EU to resolve the nationalistic problem of an Albanian minority has evaporated.

Thus, the pressure to resolve the name issue is becoming a moot point.

Major change. Major release of pressure and stress.

I believe Macedonia will become the regional hub of the Balkans and beyond (a total market of 650 million people).

Such a hub is needed. At one time it was Athens, and before that Beirut. Neither is functioning well today for separate reasons. So global corporations are looking for a city in which to base their regional headquarters in the Balkans. Skopje is working on providing just that. The whole city is covered by wi-fi. Local transportation is easy. Government bureaucracy is minimal. Corruption is non-existent. Air travel is easy. The Skopje airport received the award for the best European airport for a city with two million travelers a year. It is large, modern, and very efficient. Because the government subsidizes air transport, many airlines are starting to fly to and from Skopje. (One can fly for $50 to London from Skopje.)

The government has also invested large sums of money in the arts. There is a national theater and a symphonic hall. In short, Skopje does not feel like a rustic village anymore. It has become a modern, developed, European city.

I was impressed and remain so.

Kazakhstan

I was there for a lecture and did not spend much time in Kazakhstan. What I saw impressed me though. It is a rich country. You can see it from the cars that speed across the roads. Modern, expensive cars. Lots of late-model Mercedes. High-rises with modern architecture wherever you look.

It is a country rich in oil with a stable, although dictatorial, government.

If there is any correlation, my observation is that the countries that are doing well are countries where a strong (somewhat dictatorial) leader runs the government, but is not corrupt. Like Singapore. And Macedonia and Kazakhstan. My assumption is derived from the way people behave, dress, and respond to my questions.

Where I noticed apathy, pollution, and a frustrated and depressed population, was in the so-called democratic, but corrupt, countries like Ukraine and Serbia.

I do not believe democracy is the most desirable system for a country in the beginning of its lifecycle. Benevolent leadership works better and is more desirable, as long as it is not corrupt and as long as it will eventually let go of power. This follows my theory that the best leadership for any system depends on the location of the system on the lifecycle.

This has been a long report, but a very fruitful trip.

The Ukraine Uprising: Analysis[1]

Author's Note: This insight was written in January 2014. One month later Kiev exploded. President Victor Yanukuvych fled to Moscow, and shortly after that Russia annexed Crimea.

I HAVE BEEN TO UKRAINE NUMEROUS TIMES. I've lectured there, received honorary doctorates from their universities, and published books and articles in Ukrainian. I have worked with Ukrainian business executives and their managers. But in all my experience working worldwide, I have never heard of or come across such blatant, open, shameless corruption as I have encountered in Ukraine.

Corruption everywhere

Don't misunderstand. I know there is a lot of corruption everywhere. Even in the United States. Even in my home city. If you want a license to build a house in Santa Barbara you need a permit, which might take a year or more before it is approved by the bureaucracy. So you hire a middleman who used to work at the department of urban planning and who knows the ropes. He is called an expeditor, and for a fee will make sure that your request for a license is granted in less than a year. To me that is corruption… though everyone considers it a normal way of doing business.

There is corruption, of course, in every nation-state.

There is corruption of course in every nation-state. You will find it in Israel, in India, in Brazil. Name any country and you will find traces of corruption. But Ukraine is a different story. It represents a paradigm shift in the magnitude and nature of corruption; a sizable jump to a different level of corruption that places it in a league all of its own.

A government racket

I was told (but did not verify) that in Ukraine you could get a medical degree for a fee. Just pay a bribe. Same with a degree to parade as a lawyer. Or any other license. Just imagine going to a doctor to be treated and having no idea if the "professional" you see is really trained or just bought the degree. To me this is a nightmare. It is a total breakdown of trust.

But it does not end there. Government officials will not let you operate in the marketplace unless you pay a fee for protection; in this case, protection from them. In its own way this is a system patterned after the mafia. If you do not pay a significant fee monthly or annually the officials will take over your business, nationalize it, or revoke your license to operate. And in many cases the officials themselves take ownership of the business as well.

During my last trip, after one of my lectures I was told by a business leader who was in the audience how a Western bank lost its investments in Ukraine. The bank invested a significant amount of money in Ukraine so that it could finance loans. The loans were given to businesses that were either owned directly by the state, to people very close to leaders within the state, or to those who worked directly for the government itself. That kind of bias is questionable, but in Ukraine they took it one step further. The loans were simply never repaid.

It would be useless to sue in court—the courts are corrupt and in collusion with the government.

Unable to collect, the mother bank put its branches in Ukraine for sale at ten cents on the dollar. Lost billions of dollars. And who bought the bank? A member of the Ukrainian president's family.

There are other variations of the scheme. The government gives loans to the banks to finance the economy. The banks loan it to businesses owned by those government officials. The businesses refuse to pay back the loans. The banks go bankrupt and the government loses its loan, but all the money ends up in the hands of the government officials via their companies. Nice scheme, eh?

The openness with which the ruling politicians take advantage of their power to enrich themselves at the expense of the nation is mind-boggling. Anyone who is able to do so takes any assets they can out of the country, and no one in his sane mind is willing to invest in the country today. Ukraine is not going bankrupt. It is already bankrupt as a system.

Cleaning the fish by the tail

What to do?

A leading intellectual in Ukraine asked me that question; his name of course has to remain anonymous. I offered a one-sentence response: "The fish stinks from the head, but it is cleaned from the tail."

In other words, the corruption comes from the leaders of the country. They set the tone. They lead the parade. They are the cause of the stinking situation. Common logic suggests they need to be changed in order for the situation to change.

But who will change the leadership? The leaders will not change by themselves. Alas, you cannot change corrupt leaders by democratic means, by voting them out of power. Those in power will rig the votes. External sanctions do not work either. The corrupt leadership makes itself even richer during times of sanctions. They control the black market for the essential goods the nation needs. It is rumored that Slobodan Milosevic made billions of dollars importing gasoline across the border in spite of the sanctions against Serbia. Being the only supplier, he could charge a fortune.

Ukraine needs new leadership that has not been infected by corruption.

There is only one solution: Clean the fish from the tail. The people must rise in protest and not desist, regardless of the cost in lives, until they have prevailed. They must say enough is enough, take to the streets, and remove by force the corrupt leaders. To the barricades. To the Bastille.

In Davos, where I recently served on a discussion panel, I was told that the president of Ukraine threatened to shoot at the demonstrators if they do not disperse. I said I hope that he does so. The audience gasped. But shooting demonstrators, one's own nationals, will infuriate the people and make them even more committed to overthrowing the president and his party leaders. Just the way the Romanians got rid of Nicolae Ceausescu.

It needs to get worse

It needs to get real bad before it gets better.

Changing the leadership is only one step towards the rehabilitation of the system. It is not enough. You may cut off the head, but the rest of the body is still infected.

Ukraine needs new leadership that has not been infected by corruption; God forbid the new regime is cut from the same cloth as the old one. The country will slide even further into despair. It is not only money that will leave the country; anyone who can walk will flee. (Maybe it was a blessing Ukraine did not join the EU. If people had the right to move freely anywhere in common market Europe, Ukraine would soon be empty of its inhabitants that have any brain to sell.)

It is important to recognize that in an uprising the goal is not only to rid the nation of its corrupt leaders but to make sure as well that their replacements are not corrupt. The new leaders must understand that cleaning house needs to be their first priority; an end to corruption their first assigned task.

That is never easy.

I believe that bureaucracy is often the cause of corruption. "A hole in the fence calls for a thief," as a Hebrew expression says, and all countries in transition experience major disruptions that cause "holes" to emerge in the process of governance. That is called bureaucracy. People are human and some do not have the strength to resist temptation and crawl through the hole to steal. That is corruption.

The new leadership in Ukraine—if one comes into being—needs to remodel the system. To close the holes to create accountability and transparency. To remodel the present day bureaucracy rather than only punish those who continue to act corruptly. Not unlike the changes the leadership in the Republic of Georgia enacted a decade ago. And the changes the leaders of Macedonia are implementing today.

It can be done. It needs to be done. It must be done. And I pray it will be done.

Quo Vadis Now, Ukraine?[1]

IT IS SUNDAY, February 23, 2014. I am reading several newspapers, among them the *New York Times*, about the daily events in Ukraine.

I believe the commentators are missing the point. I have a different opinion. I have been to Ukraine many times for work and came back just recently after receiving my sixteenth honorary doctorate from their most prestigious university. The revolution in Kiev is not against Russia. Or to bring the former prime minister, Yulia Tymoshenko, back to power, as they seem to imply. Nor is it a revolution that erupted *because* President Viktor Yanukovych changed his mind and cancelled his promise to join the European Union.

His reversal of a pledge was not the *cause* of all the current demonstrations. It was more like the spark that ignited the fire, turning vocal dissent into open revolt and speech into action, as the people spilled onto the streets. All the ingredients for a fire were already in place.

Igniting the spark

The people in Ukraine were saturated, overcome with disgust at the unending corruption; at the dire economic conditions of the country while their government was openly stealing the wealth of the country. There was no trust or respect left for the leadership of the country.

The dissatisfaction, the anger, and the hard feelings have been building for years. All that was needed for a mutiny was the "spark," the final straw that led so many voices to shout "no more" and spill into the streets.

In my opinion the reversal of signing with the European Union was that spark. It could have easily been something else. The ground was ready. The only question was what would ignite it.

I believe President Yanukovych would not have lost his position if he had not

1. Adizes Insights, February 2014.

made that final misstep; if he had not, so to speak, added oil to the fire. When the police started to shoot at the dissenters, the crowds got committed to get rid of him. And not just the crowds—his own party voted him out of power.

Russia's choice

If I were to advise the Russian government, I would say embrace the people who are protesting. They are fighting for the right cause, to have a country free of corruption. To support a corrupt leader will not endear Russia to the people of Ukraine. Crimea, granted, has a significant Russian population, but the claim that they are in danger from Kiev is unsubstantiated.

If Russia intervenes in Eastern Ukraine, if it exploits the weakness of the West—which has no strength to defend Ukraine because of its preoccupation with Afghanistan, Iraq, Iran, and Syria—it will only confirm suspicions that Russia supports corruption, that Russia has territorial ambitions. In my judgment Russia will, in the long run, lose politically rather than gain.

As to the United States, I would add that this revolution is not pro-America. It is a demand for a healthy, honest government, one that can be respected and trusted. So to the "cold warriors" in the United States I say, do not try to turn this into a false victory. Do not endeavor to show (falsely) how you succeeded in wresting Ukraine from the bonds of Russian influence.

It will only make life more difficult for the people of Ukraine and, in the process, will impede their efforts to bring some semblance of order into their own lives. In effect, open Western meddling and confronting Russia will only add oil to the flames causing the Russian minority in Crimea to demand succession from Ukraine.

As for the people of Ukraine, their best tactic is to remain neutral. To maintain normal, friendly relations with both sides. To choose not to choose either the West or Russia. Ukraine should become the new Switzerland: several ethnic groups, several religions, all living in peace, benefiting from both sides of the Iron Curtain.

In May, Ukraine should elect governmental leaders who are not politically driven or identified with the East or the West. Technocrats without the slightest taint of corruption. Leaders who can restore order and trust, and by that I do not mean imprison the crop of corrupt leaders. Vengeance addressed to the past will only take energy away from fixing Ukraine's future.

Ukraine requires a new generation of leaders, leaders who can instill hope. A leadership that is trusted and respected by the nation.

Not East. Not West. Just Ukraine.

THE IMPACT OF CULTURE IN INTERNATIONAL CONFLICTS[1]

SOME TIME AGO I was watching a YouTube video in which General Eli Zeira, head of Israeli military intelligence during the Yom Kippur War, was testifying, and de facto confessing, why he made the mistake of not alerting the military command of the impending surprise attack of Arab countries.

He said that a major mistake of Israeli intelligence analysis was not to take into account Arab culture. The element of Arab culture he was referring to was pride.

The Arab countries were defeated and humiliated by the Israelis in the Six-Day War and the wars before. They could not live with this shame. They had to do something.

Henry Kissinger, then US secretary of state, understood this well. When, during the Yom Kippur War, the Israeli army crossed the Suez Canal and were advancing into Egypt proper, he threatened Israel with withholding further American support. He requested that Israel stop the humiliation, and that they give Egypt a way to leave the war without shame.

"When you surround an army, leave an outlet free" says the Chinese philosopher Sun Tzu. The defeat then is not such that it becomes embedded in their culture for generations to come, causing the people to demand revenge.

Crimea: Facts on the ground

Now let us analyze the Crimean situation.

Crimea was part of Soviet Union, and Crimea was given to the Republic of Ukraine in 1954 when Nikita Khrushchev, a Ukrainian, was in power in Moscow. It is populated 60% by Russians—people who speak Russian, and

1. Adizes Insights, March 2014.

identify themselves as Russians. This decision was not rejected by Russians because they were all members of the same country: the Soviet Union.

After the Maidan revolution, Kiev, in western Ukraine, without any doubt leans towards joining European Union.

Now let us talk about pride and culture.

I suggest to you that Russians in Crimea would not agree to join the European Union and turn their back on their homeland, Russia. Russian people are proud people. They have strong historical, ethnic, and cultural ties: Pushkin, Tolstoy, national songs, dances…. The Russians of Crimea will not go along with Kiev's plans for joining the EU, which may even include joining NATO.

And Russia would not allow their ethnic brothers and sisters to be swallowed by the EU. It would be totally unacceptable. It would be viewed by Russians in Crimea and in Russia proper as an act of treason against the homeland.

National pride and cultural ties play a significant role in international confrontations.

> *Russia has been humiliated with the fall of the Soviet Union.*

Russia has been humiliated with the fall of the Soviet Union. It is not that Russia today wants to have all Soviet Union territory back. In my opinion it is inconceivable. The world will not allow it. Russia simply wants to regain its self-pride. To regain its footing. To straighten its back. What do you think the Sochi Olympic Games were all about if not to regain some sense of self-esteem.

To let Crimea and its Russian population be part of the EU, which is belligerent toward Russia, is to suffer more humiliation. It will not happen. Cannot happen. They will not accept more humiliation. No way.

A different game plan

What should have happened? I sent my suggestion to a member of the new Ukrainian government, whom I have known for years and who, by the way, is certified in Adizes Methodology. I said, if you do not want to lose Crimea you must announce Ukraine will not join the EU. Period. It will be neutral.

I am aware that politics play an important role for those in power. If this provisional government wants to be elected by the Ukrainians in the western part of the country, they must say that it is their goal for Ukraine to join the

EU. But this is not the time for playing politics to stay in power. It is time to tell the truth. To look reality in the eye. To tell the people that reality: If we want to have a united Ukraine we must be neutral.

Russia cannot, I repeat, cannot afford to lower its head and accept Crimea and its Russian population going to the West. Cannot. Will not.

It seems to me that Kiev has a choice: join the EU and have the country be split, or keep the country united. But for the latter to happen Ukraine has to be neutral.

Yes, I understand international law. Sovereignty and territorial integrity are sacred concepts, but when pride and culture come into play, those legalese concepts pale in comparison.

Travel Report: Russia During the Crimean Crisis[1]

WHEN THE MAIDAN REVOLT STARTED, I published a blog post applauding the revolt and called for the impeachment, if not imprisonment, of the corrupt president. This blog went viral in Ukraine. Subsequently translated into Russian, it went viral in Russia.

I received e-mails from American friends telling me they were worried about my safety, particularly if I visited Russia now. My support for the revolution was against the official line of the Russian government, and my friends felt my dissention would put me in danger if I went.

I made the trip anyway.

Upon arrival, I found Moscow busy as usual. No evidence of stress due to the Crimean crisis. The Russian opposition was dissenting and the political climate was not much different from my previous visits.

During the course of my lectures in Russia, I met over 300 executives. I was not only in Moscow, but also in Samara, a city two hours away by air. So I had exposure to more than just the Muscovites.

Looking, listening, and learning

What did I learn?

The Russians are concerned about what the world thinks of their country. The questions constantly repeated to me were: "What do you think of Crimea? Will the world isolate us? How long do you think this criticism of us will last?"

People throughout Russia do not want to be ostracized and do not want to be perceived in the way that they were during the Soviet era. Rather, they

1. Adizes Insights, March 2014.

wish to be members of the world community. And, they are very much concerned about their economy.

Some young people I talked to even participated in a march against the annexation of Crimea. They felt all this nationalistic talk was anachronistic; they did not consider it a big deal if Russians were part of Ukraine.

Overall, the common denominator was that rank-and-file Russians were now more concerned about their material well-being and their standing in the world community (they fear they will need now more visas to travel than they had to secure before) than about political convictions.

But pride is still a major force.

It is pride that drove President Vladimir Putin to annex Crimea. He even said it in his speech: Russia would not lower its head in shame and abandon the Russian population of Crimea if Ukraine chose to join the EU. That pride itself played a major role was indicated by polls showing his actions were supported by more than 70% of the Russian population.

It is pride that drove President Vladimir Putin to annex Crimea.

Crimean annexation was not primarily meant as a means of restoring the Soviet territory back to Russia. I find Russia is not interested in geographic expansion. Russia has enough trouble with the territories it already has. It is also big enough. It was a reaction to what the Ukrainian government did. They forced Putin's hand. He had no choice but to act the way he did.

Why?

Forcing Putin's hand

Because the Crimean Russians would not join the West and NATO against their homeland. And Putin, for his part, could not abandon them. It is a matter of Russian pride, of Russians unwilling to be humiliated.

If the new government of Ukraine would have announced that Ukraine would not join the EU, there would not have been a Crimean crisis. I am convinced of this. The Maidan revolution was against Viktor Yanukoyvch, not against Russia. And, the Ukrainian government should have said this.

It is water under the bridge now, and the confrontation is in full swing. The West is sanctioning Russia and Western politicians are full of condemnation of the Russian move.

Why this attack on Russia by the West? Is it for breaking international law?

Violating territorial integrity? This certainly did not prevent Western powers from encouraging the breakdown of Yugoslavia. It did not discourage the recognition of the separation of Kosovo.

Ah, history is written by the winners. And, here, the Western powers dictate which disruptions of international law are acceptable and which are not.

I attribute the Western reaction to Crimea as a remnant of the fear dating back to the Soviet era. It is a lingering anxiety that is related to the past, a time when Soviet Communism threatened to bury us, and when its political leaders had the zeal to destroy our way of living. Old memories do not die easily.

Americans and Europeans still equate Russia with the Soviet Union, although most of the Russian populace tries to shed as much of that past as possible. They want to disassociate from it. Expanding the Communist credo is, for them, passé. However, the warmongers in the West miss the excitement of the Cold War. And, they recognize that it is easier to harvest votes when they drum on old fears.

It is time the world realizes Russia and the Soviet Union are not one and the same. I myself made this mistake as well. As a child in Yugoslavia, I learned many songs I thought were Russian (Yugoslavia at that time was aligned with the Soviet Union). When I first came to Russia, I offered to sing some of them for my hosts. They froze. They showed they were not too happy. I wondered why. "These are Soviet songs," they said, "not Russian."

Russia and America

Overall, I think that there is a peculiar imbalance in the relationship between Russia and the United States. Russians neither reject nor fear America, but Americans still remain hostile to Russia. In Russia, I find everyone is eager to learn English. Business schools that copy American business education are appearing everywhere, just like mushrooms after the rain. American culture is everywhere. American music dominates the urban environment, blaring away in every restaurant. American movies show on multiple channels on TV. Stores carry American products and young people follow American fashion.

In addition, today's Russia recognizes private property and has a stock market. Everyone is chasing opportunities to earn more. I find Russia culturally more capitalistic than the US; the eagerness to gain materialistically is overwhelming. True, the economy is dominated by several major holding companies, and economic concentration is high, but the same was true for the United States during its era of industrialization at the beginning of the nineteenth century. It will be a passing period for Russia too. And, the corruption everyone talks about will pass as well. I find there is a correlation between corruption and change. Any country experiencing disruptive, major change has some degree of corruption. It is present today in China, India, and Brazil. It will pass for Russia as it did, mostly, for the US. (Discussing why change and corruption are correlated calls for another blog.)

Culturally then, and in terms of market mechanisms, America's system has won. This Americanization will spread to the political arena, too. Just give it time.

What then is so un-American about Russia that makes it "the enemy?"

What then is so un-American about Russia that makes it "the enemy?" True, people are not free to criticize the government too much, but it is not that different from Singapore where one party dominates the scene and criticism is not welcome. Nor is China much different.

Is it the authoritarian regime of Putin? Russia has been authoritarian throughout its history. It will take some time for the Russian bear to change. But a very long period of time? I doubt it. Today's Russian yuppies were born after the collapse of the Soviet Union. It is a different generation from those who were fed Communist slogans and principles. Russia's young people do not even recognize songs from the Soviet era. And now a new generation changes not every thirty, but every ten years. So give Russia ten—at most twenty—more years and within two more generations this authoritarian culture will change. It has to. The TV, the movies, the media, the Internet will see to it. A democratic culture will spread.

An authoritarian regime in Russia does not seem to stand up either, for the rejection or the fear. Has not America supported other totalitarian leaders? So, why single out Russia so much?

Perhaps it is the human rights violation record. But let us be honest: How good is the American human rights record with the prison at Guantanamo Bay still active? Has the US not supported regimes that had a terrible human rights record anyway? How about Chile during the Pinochet regime?

The lingering fear of Communism

So, where is this anti-Russian sentiment coming from? Is it that Russia does not always support American interests and has its own political interests?

Syria and Iran would be two examples. But is it not some kind of arrogance to insist that we can follow our interests but others cannot? That whoever does not vote with us is against us? Even that does not hold as a convincing argument. China does not vote with the United States all the time at the UN Security Council, and neither does France, but they are not viewed with the same scorn or animosity as Russia.

I truly believe it is the old Western fears of Communism that stand in our way. Fears have a way of becoming internalized, and, in the process, shape our attitudes and drive our behavior even though the reasons for those fears have disappeared.

Annexation or, should I say, unification of Crimea had to happen because of the way the Maidan revolution unfolded. The American rejection of Russia because of a past that is no longer relevant only delays Russia becoming a democratic society governed by the rule of law. (I will eat my hat if Russia expands more.)

Bottom line, being in Russia during the Crimean crisis was not as exciting as one would expect. It was bloody cold in Moscow. Below zero. And my knees do not react positively to changes in weather. So, I did suffer on this trip; but I also discovered a delight I did not expect. I found a better cuisine than French or Italian and, to my surprise, better than even the Turkish cuisine, which is my favorite. It is the Gruzinian (Georgian) cuisine. It is so tasteful that it defies description. Full of tasty spices. Healthy food. Lots of vegetables. I strongly, strongly recommend it.

ANALYZING PRESIDENT VLADIMIR PUTIN'S STYLE[1]

I REMEMBER YEARS AGO reading about a research project that tried to assess the effectiveness of different styles of leadership. I was a graduate student at the time, working toward my MBA degree at Columbia University.

The experiment was built around two groups of children and two school teachers. A very stern teacher, a real taskmaster, led one group; a more laissez-faire teacher led the other. In both groups, the children had to put some toys together and the researchers measured which group was more productive.

At the end of the experiment they found conclusively that the children led by the stern, autocratic teacher produced more toys. The test was over; the results tabulated. And then something unexpected happened. When the teachers left the room the children taught by the autocrat destroyed all the toys they had made.

I was reminded of this research during my recent consulting experience in Russia.

An authoritarian at work

I was working with a very authoritarian corporate president. At every meeting he was the only one to speak. Occasionally, one of his managers or staff members would ask a question. But never, ever, did anyone in the room disagree with him or even show any discomfort with what he said.

I should add these were not some low-level executives. They were in the multi-million-dollars annual compensation level. Nevertheless, absolute silence. They never argued with him, never challenged, never disagreed.

When I developed the president's trust, I dared to coach him. I asked him if it would be okay in the next meeting to try something different. He would remain silent and give his managers a chance to speak. To see what might happen. Let us capitalize on the brains of Russian managers, I said. After all you do not use their knowledge if you do not let them speak.

He agreed.

1. Adizes Insights, April 2014.

And then all hell broke loose. I literally could not control the group. I have been able to control the cabinets of several nations, and, in more than one instance a prime minister. But, not here. The participants constantly interrupted each other, and refused to follow my rules of how to conduct the meeting. It was not group dynamics as I have known it in the past. It was chaos. The worst group experience of my life.

The president took over the meeting. He immediately screamed at everyone in the room and order returned. Instantly. Then he told me, "You see. People here are not used to working as a team. Democracy is not in our DNA."

Russia has never had democracy. Participation based on mutual trust and respect, which are the values and cultural platform on which democracy operates, is alien to its culture.

The fact is the transition from an autocratic style to a democratic style is not a simple two-step process. The transformation can even be dangerous if not done correctly. Chaos and anarchy are likely to follow. The result can be disastrous; it can lead to a dangerous disintegration.

Very powerful and dangerous

Last year, President Putin opened a seminar at which I was a speaker. I sat about ten yards from him and watched him speak. Felt his energy. I would not like to be on a dark street with him unless I knew he was on my side. The man does not smile. He vibrates energy that says: "Do not mess with me or else…." Basically, he is very powerful and thus dangerous, if he is an adversary.

People here are not used to working as a team.

How much of his style is related to his personality and how much is it a reaction to the culture that demands it, I do not know. But there is an interplay between his personality and the fact that to maintain leadership he has to act in a way that "the crowd" expects.

In Russia, they do not respect non-authoritarian leaders. The late President Boris Yeltsin is considered a clown, and people I spoke to in Russia have no respect for him. They view him as the leader who destroyed the Soviet Union. Gorbachev, who is another "friendly" leader (in style) is not respected either. Medvedev, who is open and seeks democratization within Russia, is considered a lightweight and weak.

It is Putin people respect. He is strong. He is decisive. He is tsarist.

How much of Putin's dictatorial, autocratic style can be attributed to his genes, to his innate personality, and how much is a response to what people expect, is not yet clear to me. But I believe that Putin is caught in a trap. Even if he wants to change, he cannot do it easily.

From my vantage point working often in Russia during the past two years, the West is judging him harshly, ignoring the culture within which he operates and the limitations it places on him.

PART II

✣

CHALLENGES TO THE JEWISH STATE

REACTING TO THE NEWS:
THE FLOTILLA TO GAZA[1]

THE FACTS ARE WELL KNOWN: A flotilla of boats was attempting to break the sea blockade of Gaza. Israel offered to take the flotilla to an Israeli port to check the content of the boats, to assure itself they did not contain ammunition, and, if not, to allow the contents to proceed on land to Gaza.

What was illegitimate in the Israeli demands?

Only last month it was reported that Syria provided Scud missiles to Hezbollah; missiles that can reach Tel Aviv and Jerusalem. Without a blockade Iran can and will arm Hamas to the point that Israeli life will become a continuous nightmare: terror on the streets and missiles dropping on schools; endless warfare, well supported by enemies sworn to wipe Israel from the map.

Negative world opinion

Why is world public opinion against Israel?

I am in Moscow now and the news announced that on the question of whether Israeli action is justified by its security needs, 79% responded "no."

Is the world nuts?

Why is world public opinion against Israel?

Which country in the world would allow an unchecked shipment to be carried to its enemy whose public charter commits itself to the destruction of that country, an enemy who walks its talk by daily bombarding the country?

The easy explanation is always ready and never fails to explain anything we Israelis consider illogical or unfair: anti-Semitism.

1. Adizes Insights, June 2010.

If I had the power of a magic wand, I would forbid using anti-Semitism as an explanation. Ever.

I am not naïve. I know there is anti-Semitism. I have experienced it and still do. And still I would forbid it from being used to explain our difficulties.

Why? Because attributing anything we do not like to anti-Semitism puts all of the responsibility on others, the so-called anti-Semites, and we Israelis do not have to take any action to ameliorate our continuously declining standing in the world.

An emotional reaction

Here is what I think caused the world to turn against Israel in spite of Israel having a reasonable right to inspect the flotilla. The world feels more pity for the poor, unemployed, starving Palestinians in Gaza than for the security fears of the mighty Israel.

It is an emotional reaction. Not a cold, calculating, logical reaction. The world identifies with the underdog.

The world identifies with the underdog.

Israel warned the organizers of the flotilla not to proceed because Israel would not allow the unchecked shipment to be delivered. But why did those warnings never make it to any media? I read the *New York Times* daily and rarely miss a newscast from CNN. Where were the warnings? It is a story the media likes. There is tension. Danger. Still nothing. Nada.

Where are the pictures of the Qassam missiles dropping on Israeli schools and the fear that the flotilla might be carrying more dangerous, longer range missiles? Where are the demonstrations on the streets of Tel Aviv requesting that the Israeli government stop the flotilla? Not all demonstrations are spontaneous. Many are staged by governments to get attention. Why not this time?

Where are the interviews with Israeli mothers expressing fear? How come we did not prepare the world for what inevitably happened and create some sympathy for our actions?

Israeli PR stinks, and stinks so badly that the word "stinks" does not do it justice.

The rationale in Israel

Israel has one explanation: anti-Semitism. As if saying: There is nothing we can explain. It won't work. The world hates us. Period. They won't listen.

Why try?

Another explanation is that Israel hates showing that it is weak. We have been weak for two thousand years. We will not cry anymore, ever again. We will be strong and defend ourselves and never show fear. But one who shows no fear when fear is due is arrogant, and that is what world opinion is reacting to.

How convenient to have anti-Semitism as an explanation that does not require you to do anything. And how dangerous.

Israel is ignoring world opinion to its peril. It is world opinion, sympathetic to the plight of Jews after the Holocaust, that made the world vote for Israel's establishment. It is world opinion now that will not support Israel's need for security. That can bring it to its demise.

What Can Israel Learn from the Japanese?[1]

JAPANESE CULTURE IS NON-CONFRONTATIONAL. In negotiations, for example, the Japanese always give their negotiating partner an exit strategy. They might make a ridiculous offer that has to be refused. That way, neither side feels defeated.

Here is an over-simplified example to make the point: You ask a Japanese if he would like to buy the iPhone you are using right now for a million dollars. An Israeli or a Serb or a Mexican would be furious: "Do you think I am an idiot? Why would I pay you a million dollars for an ordinary iPhone?"

But the Japanese will smile and make a counter-offer that you will have to reject. "Sure," he'll say, "and I will repay you one cent per year." Suddenly, *you* are the bad person, breaking a potential deal by taking the offer off the table. The Japanese, on the other hand, appears to have been positive and willing.

Why am I telling this story?

I am in Israel, where about half the newspaper front pages every day are devoted to debating the United States' request that Israel freeze construction beyond the Green Line (the pre-1967 borders), where the Palestinian state may eventually be located. Barack Obama's administration claims such a freeze would build the Palestinians' trust of Israel, which is essential for reaching peace in the Middle East.

This request is causing lots of political pain in Israel. The politicians on the Right, members of Netanyahu's current ruling coalition, are against such a freeze, and if Israel acquiesces to the US demand, Netanyahu's government might lose its majority in the Parliament, forcing new elections.

1. Adizes Insights, November 2010.

But if Israel rejects the idea of a settlement freeze, it will nurture the already common perception around the world that it is an arrogant occupier that is not willing to make accommodations for peace.

Perhaps a Japanese response

How should Israel react?

Well, what would the Japanese do? A Japanese politician would respond positively, but ask for some concession that the Palestinians have previously refused to make. Then it would be the Palestinians who appear to be the deal-breakers.

It has to be an action that increases mutual trust.

Israel's reaction to demands for a settlement freeze should not be "No," or even "Maybe." It should be: "*Yes*—and…" The "and" should refer to what the Palestinians must do to increase Israeli's trust in them, too.

It has to be an action that increases *mutual* trust. For instance: "Israel welcomes initiatives that promote peace. Israel will freeze new construction beyond the Green Line to manifest its commitment to negotiate a sustainable peace with the Palestinian people, as soon as the Palestinians, both in the West Bank and Gaza, show their own commitment to building trust by removing the anti-Jewish and anti-Israel material from their school textbooks, as well as material glorifying the *shahid,* and substituting messages promoting peace."

Placing the burden on the Palestinians

In other words, give the Palestinians a political hot potato—one that is just as hot for Palestinian politicians as is a concession freezing settlements to the Israelis.

The Palestinians refuse to come to the table to negotiate until the construction of settlements is frozen. Israel should play the same game, refusing to come to the table as long as the next generation of Palestinians is being educated to hate and kill Israelis.

Israel should have an active policy to show the world that it seeks peace. The Palestinians should be put on the defensive for rejecting Israel's peace initiative.

Currently, most of the world has the opposite impression: that the Palestinians appear willing; it is the Israelis who are the reluctant ones.

Please note how effective Palestinian public relations are, and how absolutely disastrous Israeli public relations are.

Israel has already retreated from Gaza. When he was prime minister, Ehud Barak made a most generous offer for peace. Despite never missing an opportunity to reject Israel's peace initiatives, the Palestinians are still believed to be peace seeking, while Israel is seen as the warmonger.

In Israel, more than 100,000 people have marched to demand "Peace now!" while Palestinians have never marched for peace. And yet Israel still appears to be on the warpath while the oppressed Palestinians want peace.

I understand that the Palestinians are underdogs and Israel is the mighty force of the Middle East. But images can be controlled. By not taking control of its image abroad, Israel is losing the PR war, the power of which, in today's environment of TV, Internet, and other media, cannot and should not be underestimated.

Israel: Left, Right, or Both?[1]

O N THE DIAGNOSIS SIDE, I am a political Leftist; I am in their corner. Israel *has* taken and settled land that was once occupied by Palestinians.

The claim the religious Jewish Right has made—that this is Jewish land because it was promised to Jews by God several thousand years ago—does not hold water for me. There is a legal principle called a forfeiture: If you do not occupy your land and do not lay claim to it for a prescribed period of time, you are considered to have abandoned it. It then becomes the property of any occupant who has lived there for another prescribed period of years. (The law is written differently in different countries, but it exists almost everywhere.) The Jews' claim to the land, based on a single Jewish family in the Galilean village of Peki'in that supposedly never left Israel, hardly justifies a right to the whole country. Nor does the fact that we never stopped praying to return, and dreamed of it for two thousand years.

Where we are and why

We took the land by war. Period. And we are not the first, nor will we be the last, to do so.

Yes, we had our reasons for taking *this* land rather than any other land. The Soviets offered us Birobidzhan; Baron Hirsch tried to settle us in Argentina; and Theodor Herzl even considered the idea of settling the Jews in Africa—but none of these alternative locations succeeded in settling the wandering Jewish souls. Only the land where our ancestors lived succeeded in doing so. For this piece of the desert, Jews were, and remain, willing to die.

> *We took the land by war. Period.*

After two thousand years of continual persecution—especially after the Holocaust—the Jewish people clearly need to have a land of their own, to

1. Adizes Insights, March 2011.

calm their suffering, weary souls. But as far as the Palestinians are concerned, *none* of this reasoning is relevant. *They* did not cause the Holocaust. They did not inflict the pains of the Inquisition either. So why should the Palestinians pay a tragic price for a problem they did not cause?

So up to here I agree with the political Left: *We* are the cause of the Palestinian tragedy. My sympathies and sense of justice cannot help but be persuaded by Palestinian pain. We should apologize. We should make reparations and pay them for whatever we took in wars, and it is simply irrelevant which side initiated that war. We claim they did by attacking Israel first. They claim they attacked because we threatened to take their land. I suggest we stop this bottomless discussion. They lost. We won. If there is going to be peace their loss has to be recognized.

So my diagnosis of the problem corresponds with the opinions of the Left.

Alternatives

But what should be done *now*?

In the "therapy" stage of consulting, in how we solve the problem, I move to the moderate Right.

Let us look at some alternatives:

We could simply reverse history and tell everyone to go back to wherever they came from. Obviously, that isn't going to happen. No one can reverse the wheels of history.

Okay, why not let all the Palestinians return to their land? Let's think about this. The Palestinians who populated the refugee camps in Lebanon almost destroyed that country. The Jordanians killed thousands of Palestinians who had accepted citizenship in Jordan and then conspired to overthrow the government. Nor are Palestinians welcome in Saudi Arabia or the Gulf states. So why should anyone believe they would be willing to live peacefully with six million Jews in Israel?

I do not believe this solution, a bi-national state, would work. Before long, the country would become another Ireland, or worse.

So the usual solutions the Left offers are not acceptable to me, although I agree with their diagnosis.

Then why not let the Israelis put up a security wall along their border and maintain the status quo? This is a temporary solution—an effective one for now, but it could not work permanently, because over time the demographics of the region will eventually render it ineffective. The Palestinians are grow-ing in numbers, and their children have no future. Their only conceivable future is to commit suicide and go to heaven, taking as many Jews as pos-sible along with them.

Furthermore, as the Palestinians grow in number, and their plight becomes worse and worse and their options ever more circumscribed, Israel is sure to become an international pariah. No one can survive the wrath of the entire family of nations.

Then how about two states? Aha! That is the solution currently favored internationally. But neither Hamas nor Hezbollah will accept it. They refuse even to talk about it, much less negotiate around it.

Hezbollah and Hamas revere Salah al-Din, who kicked the Crusaders out of the Holy Land in the twelfth century. They see Israel as another colonizer, no different from the Crusaders. And Israel must be made to leave. No negotia-tions whatsoever. Or they must let all Palestinians come back to their homes, which may not even exist anymore, and to their orchards, which have prob-ably been transformed into high-tech factories.

One common denominator

Those proposed solutions have one common denominator: Israel's enemies want us dead.

Social science has long posited that the justification for most, if not all, of our actions is survival. So who can blame us for refusing to accept a solution that would lead to our destruction? What country would commit suicide willingly?

Here, I agree with the moderate right wing: In order to survive Hezbollah and Hamas, we need to stay strong. But we will have to make do with Fatah—to make peace with them and work together to establish a Palestinian state.

"But they cannot be trusted!" some very right-wing people in Israel might say. "They will arm themselves and then attack us." To that, I say: Yes, maybe so. But I would rather fight an ordinary established army than a terrorist cell.

In conclusion, I cannot see any alternative to pursuing the two-state option while at the same time vigilantly maintaining military superiority.

I support the diagnosis of the Left but the solution of the Right.

THE JEWISH PEOPLE[1]

IT IS TYPICAL OF THE JEWISH PEOPLE to always be searching for ways to survive. That is because the fear of being annihilated is real.

In Israel, almost every single extended family has lost at least one member to violence caused by hatred. In my extended family, I count 108 who were murdered in World War II because they were Jews. That was the only reason.

The fear, and therefore the constant quest for safety, has been embedded in our genes during 2,000 years of discrimination, persecution, and outright extermination. In a Jewish mind, there is always a "What if?"

Will it ever change?

Anti-Semitism is here to stay.

I do not think so. Anti-Semitism is here to stay.

I suggest that one of the major reasons for anti-Semitism is the pain, fear, and anger that people experience during major changes such as economic, political, or social upheaval. People look for a reason for their pain, and find it convenient to identify a villain, a culprit, as the cause.

As we all know, there is worldwide economic upheaval right now. Furthermore, systems of governance are being challenged too. It isn't just socialism and Communism that have been discredited. The superiority of capitalism is also being questioned. With such profound changes comes pain, and with pain, the inevitable search for a villain. I fear we are about to experience a new wave of anti-Semitism—of historic proportions.

It is painful for me to say this, but I do not believe there is a solution to anti-Semitism. As long as there are crises caused by change, and as long as human beings continue to look for villains to punish (the simple solution), there will be anti-Semitism. To paraphrase Voltaire: If the Jews did not ex-

---

1. Adizes Insights, January 2012.

ist, they would have to be invented. The world must have its scapegoats one way or another.

Searching for survival

As we have done throughout our history, we must continue searching for ways to survive.

What to do? One solution was (and for some it still is) assimilation. Assimilation is what the Jews in Germany, prior to the war, believed would neutralize the danger of persecution. Assimilated Jews became enthusiastic and loyal members of the country's cultural and scientific leadership. But as we know, assimilation did not work. On the contrary, those who believed assimilation would protect them did not escape in time and were gassed to death.

Zionism has been another survival strategy. Zionists believe that all Jews should return to the country of their ancestors and resettle the land as a Jewish state. If the country maintains a strong army to defend itself—even, if necessary, with nuclear weapons—safety will be ensured.

I am in pain to have come to the realization that neither the Jewish state nor assimilation will be able to save us. I believe that both create a false and possibly fatal sense of security.

Israel is becoming increasingly cut off from the rest of the world, as if it were being prepped for surgical removal. And the Palestinian issue gives anti-Semites a convenient fig leaf to cover their desire to see the Jews disappear from the face of the earth. It legitimizes their hatred.

Consider: If the Zionist dream is realized and all Jews are in one place, and Israel loses one major war—the Arabs can afford to lose many wars; Israel only one—it will be its last. If Israel lost the war totally, what do you think would happen? I shudder to even imagine how the radical Muslims would handle their victory. Or consider the Iranian nuclear threat, if the Iranians do carry out their threat to wipe Israel off the map....

Is it smart strategy to put "all the eggs in one basket," in a very dangerous neighborhood?

How about assimilation?

Assimilation won't work, either. Even in America, anti-Semitism is growing, although it has not reached a level dangerous for our existence. But if another major economic breakdown occurs, as many predict, anti-Semitism in

America might grow to be unbearable, too.

What to do?

A third strategy

Historically, the Jews also had a third strategy to guarantee their survival: relocation from a less secure place to a more secure place. In Roman times, they moved as far from the center of the Empire as possible, to the outskirts—Poland, Russia—where they felt more secure. During the Spanish Inquisition in the fifteenth century, they moved to Turkey and other Muslim countries. To escape the pogroms of Eastern Europe, they emigrated to America and Australia. That is how they got that image of the Wandering Jew.

Sometimes families deliberately spread themselves around the globe—one son to America, another to Australia, perhaps another to South America. That way, no matter where the trouble burst out next, someone would survive.

Rashi, one of the sages of Judaism asked the rhetorical question: Why did the Lord spread the Jewish people all over the Diaspora? So that their enemies cannot get them easily, was his answer.

To remain flexible enough to pick up and go at the first warning, Jewish people have traditionally valued and invested in knowledge, in education. *Just in case* they had to move from one country to another, their assets were stored and carried between their ears. "You can make a living anywhere in the world as a medical doctor," my mother used to tell me as she begged me to go to a medical school. (She hardly needed to explain *why* I might need to emigrate, that throughout history Jews have consistently been ostracized and harmed. I already experienced that more than once from early age.)

Move to Israel? I do not think Israel has the capability to secure our long-term survival. The Muslim countries are too numerous around it. In Australia, like America, anti-Semitism is on the rise.

Quo vadis, Jews? Where to?

Asia—China, India, Japan—seems the next outpost for the Jewish people where anti-Semitism is unknown. In addition, China and India are booming economically, and in a boom anti-Semitism is low.

Author's Note: As I re-read my own essay above, I pray to God that I am wrong. That anti-Jewish hatred will stop. That we will not have to move around the globe in search of shelter. That we will be able to live in peace in Israel. That we will be members of the family of nations like any other nation without this unending fear of the next Holocaust. Amen.

Will Israel Attack Iran?[1]

Author's Note: This insight was written in 2011, barely three and a half years ago. Thus far my prediction has proved wrong—and the world in the Mideast has churned and churned again, in Syria, Iraq, and with the appearance of ISIS. The lesson learned might be to take care with Mideast predictions. The area is too volatile, too unpredictable.

IT IS NOT ADVISABLE TO PREDICT anything in this turbulent world. One cannot even trust what one reads in the newspapers or hears in the media. But I can't resist analyzing the current standoff between Israel and Iran, and sharing my insights, wrong as they may be.

I believe Israel will attack Iran.

Why attack?

Not because an attack would stop Iran from developing nuclear weapons—when there is the will there is the means, and Iran has the will. Not because an attack would stop a nuclear Armageddon by preventing Iran from using nuclear weapons—just the opposite. An attack might start a devil's dance with disastrous repercussions not just for Israel, not just for the Middle East, but also perhaps for the whole world.

How so? Iran is not alone. It has supporters in the Arab-Muslim world who would seek revenge, and not against Israel alone. Iran has already announced that if Israel were to attack, Iran considers the United States an accomplice. (Israel will be using US-made planes, no? And Israel has forever been an ally of the US.) Iran and its Muslim supporters will release an unprecedented wave of terror on US soil and, for that matter, on Europe too. What a great excuse to attack the West with no restraints. I would not take this threat lightly.

So, why does Israel not wait and see whether Iran will, indeed, launch an attack? True, it might cost several thousand lives if Iran moves first, but if Israel attacks first and Iran's revenge is unleashed against the Western world, there might not be fewer casualties.

I have spoken with some knowledgeable Iranians who told me that Iran is too smart to use the bomb. It is a poorly kept secret that Israel, too, has a

1. Adizes Insights, February 2012.

nuclear arsenal and could strike back. Iran knows there will be retaliation and it will cost them too many lives to deliver on their threat. The bomb, those Iranians claim, is a defensive vehicle, not an offensive vehicle.

So why would Israel attack first?

Because of the mythos of "never again!"

The memories of the Holocaust are still driving Israeli military and foreign policy: "We will never again be taken like lambs to the slaughter. Never, never, never again." It is like a mantra many Israelis repeat when asked what Israel should do about Iran. It is what children in Israel learn even as kindergartners. It is an oath most Israeli select military units take when graduating from basic training.

This is the conclusion one arrives at in history classes in Israel: We are not Diaspora Jews anymore. When attacked we will not suffer quietly anymore. We will fight back. Israel applauds Mordechai Anielewicz, who led the Warsaw Ghetto Uprising during the Second World War. There was no chance the revolt would succeed, but he and his people would rather die fighting than wait to be slaughtered. Israelis climb Mount Masada and identify themselves with the Jewish zealots during Roman times who committed suicide rather than die as slaves.

I believe the decision to attack will not be driven by logical, cold, rational deliberations but by this cultural mythos Israelis cannot resist.

Neither Prime Minister Benjamin Netanyahu nor Ehud Barak, his defense minister, would like to go down in history as the leader who behaved like Diaspora Jews, who sat there watching the Iranian threat advancing like a dark cloud rather than proacting against it. Even if taking action would bring disaster upon their country. Even if waiting and doing nothing is the more rational decision.

And what will the United States do?

It is in the United States' interest to see Iran lose its capability to have a nuclear arsenal but, at the same time, to appear to be against military action and for peaceful diplomatic efforts instead.

Why? In order not to turn the wrath of the Muslim world against it. Yet the US will quietly encourage, or at least not prohibit, Israel from launching an attack. Let Israel do the dirty work. The US and the rest of the world will keep their distance and purity.

After the attack, after its interests were well served, the world can accuse Israel of being aggressive, irrational, a warmonger, etc. It is nothing new. Jews have been used as scapegoats before....

Ah, the dirty politics.

Are the American and Israeli Strategies Diverging?[1]

A HEN AND A PIG WERE GOOD FRIENDS for many years. One day the hen had a great idea: "Let's open a restaurant and serve an American breakfast of ham and eggs, and make some money," the hen said excitedly.

"Great idea," said the pig, "except that what is only a contribution for you is a total sacrifice for me!"

The stakes are not the same for the United States and Israel if Iran develops operational nuclear weapons.

On numerous occasions, radical Iranian clerics have expressed their morbid intention to wipe Israel off the map. Can Israel take a chance and assume they won't? What price would it pay if its assumption turns out to be wrong? Will Israel be willing to take the chances of a second Holocaust?

When you do not have a choice, you do not have a problem to ponder, you just have to act; and Israel has no choice. It has to do whatever it takes to stop Iran from building a nuclear arsenal.

For the United States, however, to attack Iran—to open a third front—the stakes are too high. To be openly belligerent toward Iran, and to support Israeli actions against Iran, has the added political cost of further angering radical Muslims.

So, what is the best strategy for the United States? Tell the world that you are for diplomacy, for continuous negotiations. Send Secretary of Defense Robert Gates to Israel and have him tell the media that he has strongly suggested to the Israeli leadership that they should have patience and do nothing, etc. But do nothing drastic, like threatening sanctions, to stop Israel from attacking Iran.

1. Adizes Insights, March 2012.

The United States will appear in the world's opinion polls as peace loving, while Israel, fearing for its existence, will do what needs to be done.

This would be a perfect scenario for the United States, but a public relations disaster for Israel. Once more, Israel would be seen as the aggressor, the uncontrollable bully of the Middle East, the ungrateful ally who rejects the advice of its benefactor and decides to use force, even though the mighty United States claimed there was no need to do so.

Not heeding the US's prescriptions will weaken any claim Israel might try to make that it had to act. Israel's unilateral action will enormously weaken Israel politically, and American Jewry will be immobilized to support Israel because it will fear being accused of lack of allegiance to the US.

> *Israel already has very few friends left among the family of nations.*

Israel already has very few friends left among the family of nations. The Left worldwide harbors anti-Israeli sentiment because it always supports the underdog. Anti-Semites are enjoying endless opportunities to justify their hate. The only supporters Israel has left are radical Christians. They support Israel because according to the Bible, God promised that land to the Jews. Their support is solid, because God's promise is solid—but how many votes do radical Christians have now? Didn't their political power wane after George W. Bush left the White House?

The above scenario calls for Israel to massively increase its strategic public relations efforts. Israel, however, is not particularly preoccupied with the anti-Israeli sentiment. Israeli strategic PR is less than mediocre. They preach to the choir, making their presentations mostly in synagogues.

Why is that?

When, years ago, I tried to convince a very senior member of the Israeli cabinet to invest major resources in strategic PR, he said, "It won't help. They'll hate us anyway." And he was not alone in feeling this way.

For thousands of years, the Jewish people have been accustomed to being rejected, criticized, and hated. So what else is new? Jews just accept rejection as a fact of life and do not allow it to hamper what they are doing. But right now, this imperviousness to criticism and hatred could be fatally dangerous.

Isolated, Israel will be a pariah to the world. I can imagine not only academic and cultural isolation, but also economic sanctions being levied against Israel.

Israel is in a lose-lose situation: lose if it acts, and lose, maybe even more, if it does not act.

Israel Must Be Strong[1]

No, THE TITLE OF THIS BLOG is wrong. Israel should be *very* strong. No, no. Wrong again. Israel must be so strong that its enemies can never contemplate an attack on the Jewish state.

Why? I am watching the news. President Bashar al-Assad murdered sixty people who were standing in line at a bakery in Syria. They were waiting to buy bread. These were Syrian citizens. Non-combatants. If Assad is capable of punishing his own people in this way, what would the Syrians do to Jews if they succeed in conquering even a part of Israel?

> *There is no respect for life in that neighborhood.*

But, it is not just Syria or Assad. What happened in Lebanon? What is happening in Gaza to anyone who disagrees with Hamas? And what about the manipulative use of children? Sending them to kill themselves as *shahids*. Using children as human shields.

And what about Iran? What happens in Iran to women who are not fully covered walking the street?

And did not Saddam Hussein attack Iran with chemical weapons?

And what happened, and is happening, to Coptic Egyptians (i.e. to those Egyptians who are not Muslims)?

Look what is happening in Pakistan, in Afghanistan. Death, killings, and beheadings are almost a standard operating procedure.

There is no respect for life in that neighborhood.

If that is how they treat their own people, one does not have to be a rocket scientist to project how will they treat the Jewish people if given the slightest

1. Adizes Insights, December 2012.

opportunity. If any Arab nation succeeds in conquering Israel, Jewish blood will flow like a river. And who will stop them? Who stopped Auschwitz? Who stopped the pogroms?

Yes, there were righteous people who saved Jews. I was saved by an Albanian Muslim family. But is that *the* solution? To rely on a handful of "saints?"

Am I writing this blog out of fear? You bet. There is too much at stake not to fear.

ON SHARING SPACE[1]

IN MOSCOW I RECENTLY ENCOUNTERED an interesting phenomenon. Moscow is the economic, financial, trading, political, and social center of Russia. People want to live there. The price of real estate is sky high. (Moscow has the reputation of being the most expensive city in the world for business travelers.)

What happens to married couples that live in a one-room studio when they get divorced? Neither one can move out. But they hate each other. What now? They learn to live together nevertheless. I hear of situations where each of the divorced people marries a new spouse. Now, two couples share the same apartment; in some cases, share the same bedroom. They have to learn to live together or they will make each other's life miserable.

What if it is not just two couples but two families sharing the same kitchen and the same bathroom, which was quite a prevalent situation in the Soviet Union times? The same principle holds, and if someone was unruly, he or she had to be disciplined for the benefit of all. No other choice.

Why am I telling you this? Because it reminds me of the Middle East.

How to learn to live together

The Palestinians and the Israelis share the same space. Neither one wants to move out. Neither can kick the other out either. They dream about making the other one disappear, but the reality is that it is not going to happen. Ever.

So what to do? They must learn to live together somehow.

What do Russian parents do with unruly children who continue to make

1. Adizes Insights, December 2012.

havoc? The cool-headed parents must lock them in the bathroom to make life reasonably acceptable.

The families do not have to like or love each other. They just have to accept the reality that they have to share the apartment. It is really an academic exercise, which does no good, to analyze who was there first and who is the interloper. Just the opposite, it only feeds the fires of hate and undermines the probability of finding a livable solution. The fact is that they now share the same room, the same bathroom. They breathe the same air and get water from the same faucet.

Neither one wants to move out.

Making the other party's life miserable will only backfire because the other party has means to retaliate. Cool heads must take control of the situation and stop the cycle of hurting each other. Just find a way, design and agree on rules of conduct that make life livable. Not necessarily comfortable. Just livable.

There is one major reason why that might not happen although it is the logical thing to do.

Let me call it the Romeo and Juliet syndrome. The two families hate each other and are scared that their children might stop the generations-old rift and fall in love with each other and marry. Then the continuity of the "pure family blood lines" will get contaminated.

Hmm…Could this be true in the Middle East? The hate serves both parties. It prevents the kids from getting along. Mixed marriages will contaminate the purity of Jewish lines or Muslim lines. God forbid. So better keep fighting. Until Romeo and Juliet commit suicide. Is that our future?

What Should Israel Do?[1]

IRECEIVED THE FOLLOWING RESPONSE to my last blog post, "Israel Must Be Strong," (reprinted on page 78 of this book) from Faysal, a Lebanese businessman who lives and works in Nigeria. He is a great friend of mine, and has been a practitioner of the Adizes Methodology for a long time. It is worth sharing with all of you.

A letter from a friend

Here is what Faysal wrote:

> I do not have any issue with the need for Israel to be and remain strong, as long as this strength provides them the courage to make a just and lasting peace with the Palestinians and their Arab neighbors. As for the respect to life, need I remind you of the massacres that the Israelis committed against the Palestinian people in the '40s and continue to do so, the numerous invasions on Lebanon, especially the brutal attack in 2006. It was not the Palestinians who were responsible for Auschwitz! So why continue to inflict so much harm on these people…? Israel occupied Palestinian land, drove the Palestinians from their homes, continues to build settlements on their land, and to practice the worst manner of Apartheid, treating them as third-class citizens! Where has the Jewish conscience gone…!

Here is my reply:

> Dear Faysal:
>
> My heart hurts for the Palestinians. Trust me. I mean every word here. On my blog I have said, and I repeat, they should have a state: Palestine. Israel should offer to pay reparations for all the land it occupies. And those billions of dollars should go towards building the Palestinian economy.

1. Adizes Insights, January 2013.

What to do, but also how to do it

It is not because Israel has done wrong. That is irrelevant. We need to improve the life of Palestinians and help them build their economy. And we should say "sorry." Truly apologize, with all our heart. Because you are right: The Palestinians did not cause Auschwitz. So why are they the ones to suffer?

I do not know if you ever read those blog posts.

The problem is that the Palestinians have not shown real, honest interest in making peace.

Hundreds of thousands of Israelis march, calling for peace now. Israeli Prime Minister Yitzhak Rabin was murdered by an extremist because he was promoting the idea of peace. In comparison show me even one demonstration in any Palestinian territory or in any Arab country calling for peace. Mahmoud Abbas speaks of peace, but only in the English language. In Arabic, he calls for the destruction of Israel. Hamas and Hezbollah have the destruction of Israel as their announced goal.

I believe the Arab leadership is competing to see who will be the modern-day Salah al-Din. He was the great Arab leader who chased the Crusaders out of the Holy Land.

You mention Apartheid. Really? Do you know how many Arab members of parliament there are in Israel? Members of the Supreme Court? Ambassadors? Show me one Jew who can even live in an Arab country today, much less occupy a public office.

Who here is practicing apartheid?

To test who really wants peace, let us create a scenario and see what happens. Assume Israel destroys all its arms. All of them. Possesses no weapons... What will follow? Without defense, the Jewish people in Israel will be murdered. Every single one of them. Do you have any doubts about this?

If the Palestinians destroy their arms, there will be peace. Don't you agree? I am sure Israel will not see this as an opportunity to attack its neighbors.

Who really wants peace?

Israel offered an exchange of territories. Israel retreated from the settlements around Gaza and left buildings and agricultural farms intact for the Palestinians. And what happened? Every single building was destroyed. All agricultural farms were destroyed. By Hamas. Why?

Who wants peace?

Yes, Israel took land and caused the Palestinians to lose their homes. And the Palestinians did not cause Auschwitz. Yes, they are suffering. Yes, they lost their homes. Their land. Yes, they are victims. It is unfair, unjust. True.

But more Jews were expelled from Arab countries than Arabs left Palestine. As a result of a war, there was an exchange of population. It happens all the time. Except the Jewish refugees of Arab lands settled in Israel while the Palestinian refugees are being kept by their brothers in Lebanon and in Jordan as lifetime refugees in camps.

No sympathy for Israel

I believe the Palestinians have a field day in world opinion because of anti-Semitism. No other refugees have had as much sympathy as the Palestinians. Their propaganda succeeds because it rides on waves of anti-Semitism.

Israel moves thousands of families from the border with Gaza to give the Palestinians space. The world does not acknowledge this, does not give Israel any credit for its action. Israel is attacked by hundreds if not thousands of missiles landing on schools and children and civilians. Indiscriminately. How does the world respond? Not one demonstration in any nation, among any people, to show disdain for what Hamas is doing. But when Israel bombs the sites where the missiles are being fired from, Israel is accused of aggression.

I believe the anti-Semitic world doubts that there should be a Jewish state. It hurts me to say this: They would rather have us dead. I believe so. Yes I do, Faysal.

I travel the world. I observe and listen. There is a lot of jealousy. And hatred of Jews. A widespread desire to see us suffer.

Last, you are talking about Israel building settlements. Israel should stop building new settlements in what might become a Palestinian state, as a trust building exercise.

I am all for it, but the Palestinians should embark on trust building exercises too. How about changing the textbooks they use to teach children to hate Jews. To stop training little kids to embrace martyrdom.

I would say, if I were the Israeli Prime Minister, we will stop building settlements when you stop training for hate. Okay?

As Golda Meir said, "Peace will come when the Arabs will love their children more than they hate us."

Best to you, Faysal. There is nothing more I would love than to have peace. And soon. Inshallah.

President Obama's Visit to Israel[1]

THEORY: CHANGE IS CONSTANT. That means a situation does not stay the same. The rule, however, is that if it does not get better, it gets worse. But in order to make something better, an effort is required. Without effort, change will still occur, by default for the worse.

Practice: The situation in the Middle East.

Time is not working for either the Israelis or the Palestinians. No peace talks. No improvement. A downward spiral for each side.

But time is working against Israel, too.

The Palestinians refuse to come to the table to discuss peace. The Israelis continue to expand their settlements. And it becomes increasingly difficult for a Palestinian state to emerge.

Maybe the Palestinians hope that international pressure will force Israel to withdraw its settlers from the West Bank. This, it seems, is the Palestinian dream. But it is also an Israeli nightmare: hundreds of thousands of religiously driven settlers relocating by force back to the Green Line, the borders of 1967.

Won't happen. Cannot happen. Israel can stand international pressure. The Jews have a history of persecution and pressure that stretches over thousands of years. Israel can stand pressure because it is part of the Jewish culture and psyche.

Everyone is losing

In the meantime Palestinians continue to lose ground.

But time is working against Israel, too.

Ruling the Palestinians in the West Bank is undermining Israel's culture.

---

1. Adizes Insights, March 2013.

Racist incidents are increasing. Hatred of Palestinians is a mere reflex. Eventually Israel will be a country defined by cultural apartheid, if not of political or legislated apartheid. The result is that over time Israelis will lose their Jewish soul; lose their connection to values that promote the spirit of *tikkun olam*, making a better world. Its political culture has come to rely on force to survive. And within Israel itself aggressive behavior has increased exponentially.

Not a pretty picture, and it is getting uglier.

An outside intervention like a US ultimatum is not workable either. The involved parties have to make peace themselves or the peace will not be sustainable.

The discussion outlined above spells out *why* the two parties must initiate a process to find a solution. With President Obama flying to the Middle East there is a renewed opportunity to grab onto and effect change.

Is there a winnable strategy?

What to do?

Israel should unilaterally announce a peace initiative. Why should Israel take the initiative? Because today Israel has been defined by the nations of the world as the one behaviorally not wanting peace because the Israelis are expanding the settlements, claiming land on the West Bank, and creating scattered pockets that make it impossible for the Palestinians to build a cohesive state. In this scenario the Palestinians appear to be the victims. They are the beneficiaries of the world's sympathy.

If Israel seizes a peace initiative, it might effect some change in perception; a turning around of international public opinion.

What should the Israeli peace initiative be? Why unilateral?

This brings us to the *how*: Israel should announce its peace initiative as a welcome message spurred by President Obama's arrival in the Middle East. Since it will be unilateral, there is a chance it might gain some positive traction with the president.

But it is the content of the proposal that is central. First, Israel should declare that it will stop the expansion of its settlements horizontally. (It will continue vertically into high-rise buildings because of the growth of population through natural reproduction.) It will cease territorial expansion, *but only if,* and as soon as, the Palestinians stop educating their children to hate Jews. Their textbooks have to change and hatred in the media must be prohibited (and punished) by law.

Why should the initiative be conditional? Because this is the Middle East. The culture here is like a bazaar: If you give something you must get something in return. Otherwise you are perceived as being weak.

That is the mistake Israel has made repeatedly in the past: Offering unilateral concessions without requiring an equivalent response. For instance, Israel withdrew from Gaza, and negotiated the Oslo Accords, all in the hope that these acts of goodwill would promote peace. But Israel did not request a specific commensurate sacrifice from the Palestinians.

> *Israel, in short, has to offer trust-building initiatives.*

It is like saying: "I will give you real assets if you promise to stop beating me." A very Diaspora Jewish response, which the Palestinians see as weakness. In the Middle East, weakness is an invitation to ask for more in bazaar negotiations. The response by militant Palestinians to Israel's withdrawal from Gaza was to send thousands of missiles into schools in neighboring Israeli cities.

Israel should offer to stop building when and if the Palestinians stop promoting hatred. It is a form of quid pro quo. (Demanding that the Palestinians recognize Israel as a Jewish state was asking too much, in my opinion.)

The next step

If this first proposal succeeds, the next step could be for Israel to offer that it will be punishable by law to refuse to sell real estate to Arabs who want to move to a Jewish neighborhood. In exchange the Palestinians will agree to punish by law any Arab who refuses to sell his land to Jews. Again, quid pro quo.

And beyond that? Israel could offer to pay for any land that was owned by Palestinians before the war; but that money must be invested in joint Israeli-Palestinian economic endeavors.

Israel, in short, has to offer trust-building initiatives, but in the process insist on trust-building responses from the Palestinians. Put the shoe on their foot. Let them be the one to say "no" to peace initiatives.

The solution lies in the process of finding the solution. The shift should be towards a process that, step by step, seeks a workable but limited goal. Slicing the salami one slice at a time. No one can swallow the whole salami in one bite.

And Obama's visit is a perfect time to start the slicing.

PART III

❖

CHALLENGES
FOR THE
UNITED STATES

President Obama: Where Is He Heading?[1]

Author's Note: I published this insight in 2010. Much has changed, but I believe it still holds up.

"HOW THE TRAILBLAZER OF 2008 became the stymied president of 2010" was the headline on *Newsweek's* cover on February 1, 2010.

I believe I have an explanation, and it has a lot to do with my lifecycle theory of organizations. (For more information on lifecycles, please read my book *Managing Corporate Lifecycles,* [Santa Barbara: Adizes Institute Publications, 2004.])

The emerging roles of government

In the 1930s, I suggest, the United States was in the Adolescent stage of its lifecycle. A combination of factors, from Keynesian economics to the stock market crash in 1929, had legitimized government intervention in the form of the New Deal. Those changes caused the (A) role to grow, making possible the transition to Prime in the 1950s.

In the 1930s, I suggest, the United States was in the Adolescent stage of its lifecycle.

It was a healthy transition. The growing (A) did not stifle the (E)ntrepreneurial spirit because the market economy was still very vibrant. The size of the market was vast enough for entrepreneurial maneuvering, and the relative independence of the states kept the federal government's power somewhat in check. Furthermore, the principles and practice of government intervention were still, metaphorically, in diapers. Finally, the electorate's continual lurching from Republican to Democratic administrations and back again temporarily retarded the rapid calcification of (A).

Nevertheless, (A) grew. Government expenditures as a percentage of the GNP were growing exponentially, and regulatory legislation began to eat up the majority of the legislature's time and effort. It was inevitable; the rate of change continually accelerated requiring government regulation.

Between the 1930s and the 1960s, this growing role of government was functional, enabling the system to cross from Adolescence into Prime. From that point on, however, the growing (A) caused the system to start aging.

An aging process

The aging process was not linear. Technological innovation—first the computer revolution, then the internet explosion, and now green initiatives—kept (E)ntrepreneurship alive and kicking. Nevertheless, (A) grew steadily, and it had to, because of the rate of change.

As the system continued to age, it became less and less manageable. Its chief executive officer, the president, increasingly lost control.

How could the president lose control just when government was becoming a behemoth?

Who was in control, the horse or me?

This reminds me of an experience I had years ago. I was scheduled to deliver an afternoon lecture at a management conference at a hotel retreat. The retreat had horses for hire, so I decided to rent a horse that morning. It did not take me too long to realize that the horse had been doing this job for a very long time. It knew the path by heart and could tell when the hour was up without reading a watch. I tried to make it gallop up a hill. It went two steps off the path and stopped; then it returned to the path. I tried to make it gallop *down* a hill. (Please notice that I was already compromising.) Still, no willingness to cooperate. This time the horse directed its ears forward as if to warn me: "Just get on that path and don't make waves."

Who was in control, the horse or me?

For the rest of the hour I acted like I was in control, but I let that darn horse take me back to the barn on the path it knew perfectly well.

That is how presidents probably feel when they finally get elected. Running for the presidency, they have a vision, they have a plan and a desire to make change, but once they get into the White House, once they get "the power," the situation is different. Now they have to make the government function and the legislature cooperate. Meanwhile, the bureaucracy and the congress are used to doing things a certain way. Changing how they work and how they cooperate—if they cooperate at all—takes more than just wishing.

The United States as a system is aging. It is increasingly becoming "HQ heavy," and government expenditures as a percentage of GNP are skyrocketing.

Where are we now?

Where is the United States on the lifecycle now? Beyond Stable, starting to decline toward Aristocracy, with some early signs of "Salem City," the Recrimination stage.

When a system is in the first stages of aging, what it needs is (E) and (I), change and the promise of integration—and that is what Barack Obama was "selling" that the voters bought. That is what gave him the image of a trail-blazer. He got elected by projecting that he would do what was necessary to turn the aging system around and pull it out of its decline.

In other words, Obama got elected by promising to gallop uphill. But, having very limited political experience, he did not realize how difficult it is to make an aging horse gallop. He took too much on himself: health care reform, on top of having to deal with Afghanistan and Iraq and Iran, as well as resolving the credit crisis, which was sinking the economy. It was too much to do, and he promised too much.

His solutions, however, all tended to increase the role of government—which meant more (A) and further acceleration into aging. When that happens, people expect (P), results, which he could not deliver.

The result is that his popularity is sinking rapidly in the polls—to the point where he may soon be regarded as a lame-duck president, not in the last year of his presidency, but already in his second year.

I suggest to you that this was all predictable. The United States is in decline, in the aging stages of its lifecycle, approaching the Recrimination or Salem City stage. And what happens in Salem City in Arthur Miller's famous play *The Crucible?* A witch-hunt. Instead of addressing their systemic problems, people start to look for villains, believing that if they sacrifice their leaders (or refuse to reelect them), a new leader will be able to do what it takes.

Changing the system

What is needed is not a new rider but a new horse. We need to change the system. Changing presidents does not make the necessary difference. No elected president, I suggest to you, will look good in polls from now on. The polls gauging the popularity of a president are going to look worse and worse, and there will be earlier calls for his or her impeachment. Why? Because we are at the stage of the lifecycle where our desperate impulse is to sacrifice our leaders no matter what they do.

If my analysis is right, what do we need to do? We need to reengineer the system. I am not talking about more or less government, but something different: a new, modern capitalist system, based on cooperation between management and workers; a new way to control management, not only by absent stockholders but also by working insiders—the employees.

And that is nothing short of a revolution.

President Obama is not a bad president. Hopefully, it will be a peaceful revolution. The grassroots Tea Party movement, which recently sprang up in opposition to Obama's plans, chose its name from the Boston Tea Party, an act of defiance against Great Britain that began the American Revolution. Perhaps subconsciously, we are preparing ourselves for the major change that needs to happen.

But in order to reengineer the system, we will need to slaughter some sacred cows that are blocking our ability to advance. We are still stuck with the religion of adversarial relations—unions against management, managers against each other—that penetrates organizational dynamics.

As we become increasingly interdependent, we need to become increasingly collaborative. As of now, we are interdependent but competitive. And that needs to change. But that change cannot happen without a major break with the existing system. The credit crisis, as dire as it was, may just have been an early indicator of things to come.

President Obama is not a bad president. He simply was elected at a time when no president could survive the frustrations of the populace, the difficulty of making changes within the enormous bureaucracy that he heads, and the stain of dirty political maneuvers that politicians routinely use to remain in power.

He did not create the river, but he sure is getting wet swimming in it.

Obama: A Performance Review[1]

DURING THE 2008 ELECTION for the US presidency, whenever I lectured on the topic of organizational lifecycles I would ask the people who attended my lectures where they thought the United States was in its lifecycle? There was a near-consensus that the country was on the aging side of the curve.

When was the United States in Prime? Sixty years ago, in the 1950s.

What are the signs of aging? One of the major signs is the increasing (A), bigger governmental machinery, and growing government expenses as a percentage of GNP.

An aging system

In my writing about lifecycles, I have often said that the increase in (A) that occurred in the United States during the 1930s was a desirable change,

As a system starts to age it is also falling apart.

one that took the country from the Go-Go stage through Adolescence to Prime. But, as usual, what is desirable at one stage of the lifecycle can be dysfunctional at other stages. The (A), the interventionist role of government, legitimized by Keynesian economics, mushroomed and became a cause of aging.

As a system starts to age it is also falling apart. The first obvious signs of disintegration could be seen in the campaign slogan for Richard Nixon's 1968 presidential election: "Bring us together."

Typically, as the system ages people look for leadership that will provide both (E) and (I). That is what Barack Obama promised, and he was elected—

1. Adizes Insights, September 2010.

to drive a car heading downhill without brakes.

How well has he done?

He is definitely trying to change the system, and, predictably, as Machiavelli pointed out, if you want to be hated try making big changes. Obama is getting more hate than any previous president in my lifetime. George W. Bush was despised; Obama is hated. To judge by the media, he cannot do one thing right. Is it only because he is making change happen, or is there more to it?

A quick solution: Attack the leader

In my work managing corporate lifecycles I have seen that when a system approaches the Recrimination stage, an advanced stage of aging, people attack their leaders. They are experiencing pain, but instead of analyzing what is wrong with the system that is causing the pain, they personalize the cause and attack their leaders.

The next president will have it even worse.

I suggest to you that no matter who was elected—John McCain, or any of the other presidential contenders—every one of them would by now be in the same "soup" Obama is in: criticized endlessly no matter what he or she did.

The next president will have it even worse. His polls will plummet faster, and even sooner, than Obama's.

Obama is trying to fix the system. Even if you do not agree with his efforts, you must recognize that he is acting. If he did not act, he would be criticized even more. He is in a no-win situation: If he acts, he is criticized regardless of what action he takes; and if he does not act, he is criticized for his aloofness. In other words, the criticism of Obama is generated not by his actions but by the United States' location on its lifecycle. And it will only get worse.

If my analysis of the United States' position on its lifecycle is correct, then in the not-so-distant future we will see unrest, breakdown, fighting between the haves and have-nots, riots, and the rise of anti-Semitism.

Cutting the National Deficit[1]

THE COUNTRY IS IN TURMOIL. The national debt of the United States is, to put it in simple words, HUGE—huge enough to worry even politicians. National leaders are saying things like: "I am not worried about my grandchildren or my children anymore. I am worried about us, now."

It is not difficult to understand how the debt was created: The government is spending more than it is collecting. To stop the debt from increasing, the executive and legislative branches of the government have to agree on how to increase revenue (i.e. taxation) and/or how to cut spending.

It's that simple, right? That is what corporations, families, and even individuals struggle with.

Not simple at all

A high percentage of divorces occur because the couple cannot agree on which expenses to cut, or on where and how they should increase the revenues. If the issue is not addressed in one's personal life, the result is often homelessness.

The problem is not simple and mistakes are made. To cut expenses you can either cut *what* you do or *how* you do it. You can cut (P) or (A).

Cutting the *what* means, in the case of corporations, to cut the services provided to clients. This is what we're seeing right now on some airlines. Have you noticed how long the lines are at the airline check-in counters? Have you experienced the decreasing quality of meals served on your flights? The service is getting worse and worse. And to increase revenue, the airlines are focusing on *what* they provide, charging for baggage and for anything else they used to include for free.

1. Adizes Insights, August 2011.

Cutting the *how* the (A), would mean cutting the bureaucracy, the layers upon layers of managers, vice presidents, assistants, and support functions that, over time, mushroom in corporations as they age on the lifecycle.

What is happening now, as the government struggles with the need to cut government spending?

The government is making the same mistakes that many corporations do: Instead of cutting fat in order to lose weight, they are cutting the muscles, cutting the services government provides, like education, Medicare, defense, social services, and Social Security (the age at which people will be entitled to receive benefits will go up).

What about the money spent on administration, i.e. government employees? Not those in direct service like social workers, policemen, and teachers, but the myriad supervisors, coordinators, assistants, chiefs, and deputy chiefs? All those in between those on the "firing line" and the president of the United States?

Do you have any idea how big the staff of the White House is today? Four hundred and fifty-four people. Do you know how big it was during the Eisenhower administration, not too long ago, in the '50s? One hundred and thirty-eight. That's a 300% increase. Some more numbers: In 1946, there were 6,000,000 people on government payroll. As of 2006, there were 19,734,000. That is about a 330% increase.

Granted, the government expenditures are growing because the government is taking more and more functions upon itself. Expenditures, as a percentage of the GDP, show this. The National Income and Product Accounts report by the Bureau of Economic Analysis shows the amount spent on "the government" as an entity comprised roughly 24.25% of the GDP in 1961. By 2003 it became 31% of GDP, a 33% increase.

One important detail to understand

But here is what is important to know: I suggest to you that the administrative component of the "government machinery" is growing the most. Why do I assume that? Because of my knowledge of the lifecycle theory. (See my book: *Managing Corporate Lifecycles* [Santa Barbara: Adizes Institute Publications, 2004].) I suggest that the US, as a country, is starting to age and, with aging, the administrative subsystem, in this case the government (which includes federal, state, and local levels), as a percentage of the total expenditures, grows disproportionately. It is analogous to the fat we increasingly accumulate as we age, fat we find increasingly difficult to get rid of.

The problem, then, is not the deficit but what is causing the deficit. And what is causing the deficit is expenditures on a mushrooming bureaucracy. Cutting services rather than cutting the bureaucracy is the wrong solution. It analogous to a person who gets on the scale and realizes that he is fifty pounds overweight. He cuts his right foot off and gets on the scales again. It looks good now. The numbers look right.

Why do managers or politicians cut "muscles" (services) rather than cutting "fat" (the administrative layers)?

In corporations, it is easier to cut what you provide to your clients than to go to war with your own breed, the managers. There is a fear of losing control. And if all companies in your industry do the same—which is not legally prohibited, it is not considered collusion—it is not competitively disadvantaging.

In the case of a country there is a new factor: politics. The government employees cannot only strike but also vote you out of power. And how many politicians do you know who would agree to be voted out of power?

It is true that cutting services can hurt in the polls too, but politicians cut services to those who have the weakest voice—the sick, the old, and the children.

Cutting unionized, mature, voting administrators is much more dangerous; they can paralyze a country. Just look at what is happening in France.

Democracy and danger

As long as we believe in democracy and accept that the system is weak to enforce unpopular political solutions, what we are facing is the byproduct of the system we chose.

Is there a danger to democracy?

I believe so. Eventually there will be explosive anti-government sentiment, chaos—see Greece. People will prefer to be governed by someone with a strong hand who will instill some order amidst the mess.

There is a famous model about a cycle on which political systems progress (deteriorate): democracy deteriorates to anarchy, which calls for dictatorship, that is rebelled by oligarchy, only to develop into democracy, which then disintegrates into anarchy, and so on, and so on.

We sure live in interesting times. (This is, incidentally, a Chinese curse.)

ADDITIONAL SOURCES

NIPA report by the Bureau of Economic Analysis: http://www.bea.gov/national/index htm#gdp

White House Staff Information: http://www.whitehouse.gov/briefing-room/disclosures annual-records/2011

http://www.eisenhower.archives.gov/all_about_ike/presidential/White_House Staff_1953_1961/index.htm

WHEN IMAGE TRIUMPHS OVER MEANING[1]

IT IS MY OBSERVATION that we (I mean we in the United States) live increasingly in an environment where form is more important than function—how something looks is more important than its content.

The medium is the message

Take the movie industry, for instance. The technology is awesome: Cars go flying through the air, robots change form in front of our eyes, and the sounds can really shake you up. But the content is idiotic, if not downright offensive. I, for one, have stopped going to American movies; I won't waste my time anymore.

Marshall McLuhan's equation, "The medium is the message," says it all. The principle is easy to see in art forms such as television, movies, and the plastic arts, where the technology used to produce the art often overwhelms the message that art is supposed to convey. It is often seen in architecture, particularly when the form is awesome, breathtaking, while the functionality is suboptimal.

Obamacare is hardly the beginning of this trend, but it is still a step in the wrong direction.

But it is also reflected in all aspects of our culture. Look at our educational system. On one hand, we have long been experiencing grade inflation, which gives the impression that our students are excelling and our education system is achieving its goals. At the same time, the content of our education is going to hell; our high school graduates cannot read or do basic math. I once had a master's degree student who could not do multiplication without the aid of a computer.

1. Adizes Insights, September 2012.

It is reflected in health care delivery. Obamacare is hardly the beginning of this trend, but it is still a step in the wrong direction. Under Obamacare, health care will appear to be improving: People will be spending less time in hospitals, and the cost of health care delivery is going to decline. But at the same time, the actual health of the population is also going to decline as professionals are forced to surrender medical decision making to bureaucrats.

Packaging

It is reflected in the packaged-food industry. The packages are impeccable. They promise health, good taste, possibly immortality. Their success can be measured by the number of consumers who purchase the foods they are pushing. But if you consume the contents of those packages too often they may kill you.

Form over substance.

This phenomenon is reflected in politics, too. It has been argued that Richard Nixon lost to John F. Kennedy in the 1960 presidential election because he did not put on makeup for the TV debate. Can you believe that? I was aghast in 2000 when I saw Al Gore change his hairstyle to look more like Ronald Reagan's. As if that would help win votes.

This same issue is going to impact the election in November. I suggest to you that many voters will not choose between the candidates by examining the differences in their policies. They will choose by appearance: how they behave on stage; how they speak; the intonation of their voices. Their votes will be based on form, not on content.

I wish someone would interview potential voters and ask them, "What does Barack Obama stand for? What does Mitt Romney stand for?" I suggest to you that many, many voters have no idea what the candidates' policies are; nevertheless, most voters know, and are passionate about, whom they will vote into power in November.

If I am correct about that, I believe Obama will win. He appears more genuine. He is a better orator than Romney. He pauses at the right spots in his speech. He moves his hands in a way that supports what he says. His intonation is perfect. It oscillates at the right passages. Although he uses a teleprompter, you don't notice it. He is so skillful a speaker than he appears to be talking spontaneously to the person sitting next to you. He is more simpatico, more relaxed, and he smiles a lot. He moves on the stage with ease, as if dancing. He applauds the audience. The guy makes you feel comfortable. He is warm. He is not stressed. He behaves as if he has already won.

Romney, on the other hand, looks cold, distant, uncomfortable in his own skin, trying too hard to be liked. He often looks like he is reciting a speech that someone else wrote. He looks much less "authentic" than Obama.

If I am right and form prevails over substance, many will vote for Obama while having no idea what he stands for or what he will do.

Predictions are dangerous to make, but we like to make them anyway. We'll see if I am right.

Obama's Leadership Style[1]

I N MY FRESHMAN YEAR of college I took a course on international relations. In the very first class, the professor told us that interpersonal ethics do not apply to inter-country relations. What works in family therapy or community organizing does not work in international relations, he said. I do not know if he was right, but it is worth analyzing.

Obama's managerial style

Four years ago, when Barack Obama was elected president of the United States of America, several associates and I analyzed his inaugural address and tried to diagnose his style.[2] Our conclusion was that he is predominantly an (I). Now, with four years of experience, I believe my colleagues and I were correct in our analysis of Obama's management style. In this essay I wish to focus how his (I) style is manifested in his foreign policy.

Obama started his career as a community organizer, and his approach to solving problems like foreign affairs is still that of a community organizer: through (I). He is not confrontational. For comparison, try to imagine trial lawyer Alan Dershowitz as president of the United States. Or John McCain, if he had been elected. How would they approach the Muslim riots and the murder of US Ambassador to Libya J. Christopher Stevens? They would read them the riot act, that's how! What did Obama, the community organizer, do about all the anti-American demonstrations throughout the Middle East? He apologized as if it is the nation's fault that someone was practicing the right to free speech and made a movie that offends radical Muslims. He apparently believes that "being nice," being understanding and empathetic,

---

1. Adizes Insights, October 2012.

2. See "An Analysis of President Obama's Inaugural Address" on my blog: http://www.ichakadizes.com/an-analysis-of-president-obamas-inaugural-address/

is contagious. That may be true in community organizing, but it is not true in international relations.

A different set of rules

Building bridges with your adversaries, especially in the Arab world where they interpret efforts to build bridges and appease anger as a sign of weakness, apparently does not work. The rules of family therapy and community organizing apparently do not apply to international relations, especially when dealing with those that show aggression towards you.

In the Middle East the rules of the bazaar dominate. You have to haggle. If you accept their first offer, it shows you are weak and unlikely to protest if they subsequently raise prices, make new extreme demands, or ignore you.

That is where we are today with Iran, I believe.

What does a community organizer do with one member of the community who is an ally but also a source of turbulence? Israel is the case in point. The community organizer will do his best to control, isolate, and insulate the disruptive member of that community. Not support him. Why should he? He is already an ally. A community organizer will appease the enemies in order to integrate them. And that is what Obama is doing, as I see it. Instead of threats or punishment, he sends billions of dollars in aid to countries that harbor terrorists. Obama bows to the king of Saudi Arabia, a country that finances madrassas, schools that teach hatred of the West.

Obama's first trip abroad as president was to Egypt. His speech in Cairo, addressed to the Muslim world, was an attempt to build bridges. In 2010, in his speech to the Muslim world at Ramadan, he made a point of saying that American Muslims have made extraordinary contributions to the United States. One wonders what those contributions might have been, but the truth is irrelevant to an (I). He will bend in any direction if it helps bring peace and unity; textbook (I) behavior.

Please note: I am neither criticizing nor supporting Obama. All I am doing is trying to analyze his leadership style. Whether it is constructive and desirable or not, it is up to you to make that call. Maybe his (I) way is the right way in the new world in which we live, one of a global village, a global community. I did not take sides in this essay; I will in a future one.

Gun Control[1]

PARENT GROUPS, TEACHERS across the country, and the president of the United States are demanding gun control. I suggest that gun control in itself is not enough to solve the problem of mass murders.

If you walk down the main street of any city in Israel, you will notice many young soldiers about 18 to 20 years old, both male and female, all carrying rifles. It's necessary for self-defense in fighting terrorism. In spite of the availability of arms in Israel, indeed because of their prevalence, there are no mass murders.

Violence in movies and TV programs numbs us to the sight of death and murder.

I suggest that what contributes to the prevalence of shootings in America is our legacy of the Wild West. That legacy depicts and glorifies the use of guns in films and television programs. Of course there are also police procedurals, gangster films, dramas labeled as cinema noir, and the cinematic glimpses of social reality in which teenagers resort to violence and killing sprees. Our TV programs and our movies, our popular culture, project shootings with no emotion. No feeling of remorse.

Violence in movies and TV programs numbs us to the sight of death and murder. It also stirs up images and ideas for those of us who are mentally impaired or conscience deficient. Those with mental problems and with low creativity scores are fed with fantasies of glory they do not have in their real life. It is not surprising that some of the killers wear battle gear in the real-life killing sprees. That appears to be the style depicted in films and television. The idea did not magically appear out of thin air. It is not only that art imitates life. Life imitates art, too.

1. Adizes Insights, January 2013.

We have a Wild West legacy to start with. Add to it TV programming and movie industry productions that capitalize on this legacy in order to maximize profitability, and you get a culture of violence that is growing, not declining.

What to do?

We should control the possession of guns, even though that alone will not solve the problem. It is needed to arrest the problem; it might prevent some murders because it will be more difficult to get the guns. But to solve the problem we must address the cause: We need to outlaw violence in movies and television. Delegitimize it. Cease making it heroic. Make it despicable.

Here is an analogy: a swamp that breeds mosquitoes that carry malaria. Killing as many mosquitoes as possible will not solve the problem. Drying up the swamp will. But that takes time. In the meantime, you have to stop the mosquitoes from proliferating. The same applies here: to change the culture will take time. In the meantime, gun control provides symptomatic relief.

Is that it then? Unfortunately no.

Apparently we cannot do either: Controlling the guns requires changing the constitutional amendment that makes bearing arms a right of every citizen; outlawing violence in entertainment requires changing the constitutional amendment guaranteeing free speech.

Will there be political will to change the constitution? It is a double whammy—two constitutional amendments. The compounded probability that it will happen is, in my estimate, approaching zero.

All the chest beating and hair pulling over gun control will not do much unless the causes are dealt with and the constitution is changed. Which I am afraid is improbable.

What then? Carry a gun to protect yourself. Have guards at schools. I myself did not expect my analysis to end up supporting the NRA.

How much more crazy can we be?

PART IV

✿

ECONOMIC
AND
LEGAL CHALLENGES

CAPITALISM IS DYING
BEFORE OUR EYES

AN INTERVIEW WITH THE EDITORS OF *BUSINESS & BALTICS*[1]

*B*usiness & Baltics: Experts are predicting that there might be a second wave of crises; do you agree? We remember that when we last spoke, you were calling the current crisis "just a warning."

ICHAK ADIZES: I do not see any symptoms of the second wave, and I do not know whom and what it is going to hit. But I am sure that second and third waves are coming.

I am saying this based on the intense structural changes that are taking place in all spheres of life—not just in one sub-system, but in all—economic, social, political and legal. In all spheres, the situation is in turmoil. Systemic problems call for systemic solutions. Partial solutions like economic intervention do not work well anymore. It is becoming clear that we are going to need to find a new way of solving problems.

Furthermore, capitalism does not work, because it is a disintegrating force and this disintegration brings systemic problems.

Q: What is wrong with capitalism?

A: The main emphasis of capitalism is on capital. In other words, in capitalism I can invest my money without working myself. My money works for me, and I receive dividends. If I own a company and manage it at the same time, then I am in control of my capital. But in the stock exchange, a separation occurs: Those who invest the capital are no longer the controlling owners. I do not really control what I supposedly own, because I am not able to control the management of the company in which I invested. The investors do not control the boards either. If I do not agree with a company's

---

1. Adizes Insights, October 2010: Interview with the editors of the newspaper Business & Baltics, originally published, August 18, 2010. NOTE: This insight predicted the financial crisis of 2013 and those to follow.

financial results my only choice is to simply sell my shares and invest in something else.

So the loyalty of the investors is based almost exclusively on short-term profitability. And material well-being becomes the only priority. This approach has outgrown the earth's capacity to regenerate itself; the planet is becoming polluted and natural resources are getting destroyed.

At this point, the governments need to get involved. But as usual, the administrative machine that is being brought to bear is becoming too big, too expensive, and is still ineffective. People are losing their patience and starting to demand less control, since it is not working.

Because there was no good balance between control and freedom, the whole system started to function badly, and the current financial crisis was born: People took risks in order to maximize earnings, but nobody was properly controlling the total process. And now, when Obama is trying to implement some controls, many people believe that the controls are ruining the business system.

Q: Do you see any solution to this situation?

A: No, neither freedom alone nor control alone is working. Neither is a mixed system working. A third path is needed. A paradigm shift is being called for.

Communism is dead. Capitalism is dying before our eyes. The answer is not to strengthen or weaken the system of controls. A new regulatory system is needed. But today, nobody can predict what it will look like. It might be some compromise between socialism and capitalism that is able to integrate materialistic approaches with social consciousness.

But, since this new approach has not been born yet, new crises are unavoidable. We do not know which sector is going to be hit—the banking sector, real estate, or production—and that is why we are not able to predict when it is going to happen. What we do know is that currently we are fighting and solving only some consequences of some problems, but have not gotten to the roots of those problems.

The task for the new generation

Q: The question is how much time it will take to reach the roots of the problems and change the system. It took centuries to change the slave-holding system.

A: This is impossible to forecast. The only thing I know for sure is that the change will take place, and I have a few ideas about the direction in which we need to move.

If the problem lies in disintegration then the solution is in integration. We need to stop behaving according to the philosophy that "man is wolf to man." We need to stop believing that the best results are reached only through competition. The ideas of Adam Smith and his "invisible hand" do not work anymore; in fact, they lead toward disintegration. Competition has moved from the market to inside the companies themselves: Employees are fighting management, managers are fighting each other. Everybody is against everybody and they're trying to destroy each other, as if destroying others will protect them. This has to change.

> *We need to stop believing that the best results are reached only through competition.*

So a serious change in our values system should take place. The cornerstone of the new system should be cooperation instead of competition.

Another point: We need to stop measuring the progress of the society by its economic growth alone. We need to focus more on social indicators.

Q: It is difficult to believe that such a major change in thinking could take place in less than a few generations. It would require that a significant part of society reject their wealth, hold each other's hands, and start to help each other.

A: It might take a few generations until it becomes possible. But it might happen that a new generation is born that is less oriented toward materialistic values.

And it might happen even faster if a powerful crisis causes a change in behavior. Sometimes a crisis is needed in order to force important and necessary changes. "Crisis," in the languages of many nations, means "time of big changes." It is not only a threat; it is a chance for serious reconstruction.

Profiteers: A necessary evil

Q: You said yourself that materialistic society is wasting our natural resources. And we want to add: often for unimportant, even trivial reasons. What do you think about the idea of creating something that is useful for all

human beings (for example, something that strengthens our environment)?
Industry could get involved, and people would benefit from it.

A: I like the idea. But usefulness/non-usefulness is a question of attitude. For instance, people are buying Apple products like crazy. Do they really need all that stuff?

To define what is necessary and what is not is very difficult. The question is not only what do we need most of all, but also, do we need future products that are better than the products we have now, or are the current ones good enough?

Q: Economic development can be strongly influenced by speculators, who are capable of inflating or knocking down the prices of goods and resources. Is it possible to control them?

A: It is possible to increase the control by raising taxes for the high profits they are getting, but to completely get rid of them is impossible. The reason is that changes of any kind create discrepancies in the system that gets capitalized by speculators who see in them possibilities for exploitation. In order to completely get rid of speculators, you need to stop all changes, and this is impossible. Speculators are a necessary evil—possible to control, but impossible to defeat

Q: Who is going to be the driving force in future economic development?

> *I think the future belongs to the BRIC countries.*

A: I think the future belongs to the BRIC countries: Brazil, Russia, India, and China. They are highly populated. They started from a rather low level of development, and their growth is going to continue for long time. They are the markets of the future. And if you take a look, you will see that development in those countries is occurring very fast—especially in China, where they are not only consuming but also producing, and now are even starting to create products of their own. They are becoming an important economic engine.

The challenge for China is that its political system does not correlate with its economic system. In reality, the Communist Party adopted all the devices of a market economy: proprietorship, banks, stock exchange, etc. The country actually functions as a capitalist country, while still calling itself Communist.

Ultimately, I think this problem is going to be solved by the Chinese people themselves. They are a very pragmatic people whose attitude toward the future is practical rather than influenced by strong religious prejudices or ideologies.

The dissolution of the EU

Q: Economic skeptics are forecasting the fall of the euro as well as the European Union itself, based on the problems in Greece and the whole Eurozone. What is your opinion of the EU's future?

A: I do not think it is going to collapse. The globe is shrinking, new alliances are being born, and walls are falling down. There is no sense in going back to separatism, to individualism, to nationalism.

But development never goes smoothly.

After a movement forward, there is always a small movement back. This is normal and necessary for healthy adaptation to a new reality.

In my opinion, the EU will not collapse, but it will wake up and start to think about the necessary tools to make some trims. They are not going to throw out the baby with the dirty bath water. They will try to clean the water.

In my opinion, it was a mistake to keep helping Greece for all those years despite its ineffective economy. I diagnosed Greece twenty years ago and said the country was surviving only because of EU funding. At that time, I asked: How long can you rely on that support? And now, after twenty years, we have the answer. But for the EU, this only means that in the future it will need to create new methods of control.

Q: What do you think are the prospects for the Baltic countries?

A: After looking at the situation in all three Baltic countries, I believe there is a direct correlation between the level of difficulties they are facing and the level of corruption and disintegration. This is why Latvia is having the biggest challenges. The sooner you go for integration and combine your efforts, the faster improvement will come.

Q: You have traveled all over the world to advise corporations. Do you think organizations around the world have learned any lessons from the current crisis? Did any of them change their structures or cultures?

A: It is interesting that I did not notice a big difference. [Laughs.] No, corporations made some very predictable changes: They reduced costs, fired people, and became more careful, more conservative. But I did not notice any profound changes.

You can divide changes into three levels: First, to change what we do; second, to change how we do things—for example, to replace manual work by computer work. The third level is to change who we are, which is a powerful change of values.

So, during the crisis, I noticed changes of the first level and perhaps some of the second level. But most of the serious and necessary changes are in level three, and still not visible at all. Because of that, I am sure we are going to be hit by even bigger crises, which will require, but also enable, level-three changes.

The Arizona Law, Teachers' Unions, the Oil Spill, and the Greek Crisis[1]

Arizona

PEOPLE IN AMERICA are having a very emotional reaction to the new immigration law passed in Arizona, whereby police officers can stop whomever they suspect of being in the state illegally and demand proof that he is legally there. If someone is unable to show proof, he will be deported.

> *It starts with the fact that illegal is illegal. Period.*

On one side of the fence are conservatives, who support the law claiming it is high time the country began to control illegal immigration. They claim we should not tolerate or deal "softly" with people who ignore the law. Conservatives have other reasons to support their position, but it starts with the fact that illegal is illegal. Period.

On the other side of the fence are liberals, who oppose the law because it violates human rights and resembles the laws of racist regimes who used racial profiling to discriminate.

To me, it is a debate between people with an (A) style of reasoning versus those with an (I) style. President Barack Obama's position on the issue is clearly an (I) position, which is no surprise: His election campaign, his foreign policy initiatives, his method of promoting legislation, and his selection of candidates for the Supreme Court all have the (I) style as a common denominator.

But either style of reasoning points to the same conclusion: The United States is a nation in the aging stages of its lifecycle.

When the United States was in its youthful, growing stages, immigrants would arrive at Ellis Island with little or no documentation, yet within hours they would be able to cross the processing hall into the United States.

1. Adizes Insights, June 2010.

Read the sonnet "The New Colossus" (1883) by Emma Lazarus, which is engraved on the pedestal of the Statue of Liberty. Its most famous lines read:

"Give me your tired, your poor,
Your huddled masses yearning to breathe free,
The wretched refuse of your teeming shore.
Send these, the homeless, tempest-tost to me,
I lift my lamp beside the golden door!"

Does this not apply to the immigrants of today? Apparently not. What was once welcome in a growing nation becomes less welcome as the nation continues to age.

Teachers' unions

I read that the teachers union in New York has finally come to an agreement with state education authorities on how teachers will be evaluated and rewarded. The agreement says teachers will be judged by the results their students exhibit on the various standardized tests they are required to take.

But what happens when you give someone a reward or a punishment based on a measurement? Obviously, he will begin to focus almost exclusively on what is being measured. The problem is that "not everything that can be counted counts and not everything that counts can be counted," an expression attributed variously to Albert Einstein and the sociologist William Bruce Cameron.

Imagine you had a spouse who measured your love by the value of the jewelry you gave her. She might become a rich wife, but the marriage will no doubt be an unhappy one.

Education, like love, should be verified, validated, not measured. The act of measuring undermines the phenomenon you are trying to measure. The Heisenberg Uncertainty Principle does not apply only to physics.

This type of mistake, in which we try to measure how well we are doing, is due to (A) reasoning. It is for the sake of efficiency that we take this route. Measuring appears easy and is comforting. It gives the impression of being precise and thus scientific—even when it completely misses the point of why we are measuring in the first place.

This is also called the streetlamp fallacy. A man is looking for something under the bright light of a streetlamp on a pitch-dark night.

"What are you looking for?" he is asked.

"I am looking for my keys," he responds.

"Where did you lose them?"

"At the end of the street, over there."

"So why are you looking over here?"

"Because the light is here," he answers.

The inappropriate application of measurements can give us the precisely wrong answer rather than the approximately right answer.

The oil spill

Elizabeth Birnbaum, the director of the Minerals Management Service, resigned under pressure. This is the nice way to say she was fired. Former US President George W. Bush is blamed for the spill too because he fostered too many close relationships with the oil industry. And the current president, Barack Obama, admitted publicly, "I screwed up."

Was it the incompetence of the director of the Minerals Management Service, or the cozy attitude of the former president, or the bad judgment of the current president that caused the disaster to happen? Or was it the insufficient attention to safety that the BP people exhibited? Or maybe it is all of the above?

The current president, Barack Obama, admitted publicly, "I screwed up."

While all the above are potential symptoms of the problem, they are not the cause.

The cause of the problem is structural: The organization that was supposed to approve the safety of the rig was the same government agency that gave the permits to dig for oil and was the same that collected the royalties for the government.

Do you see here that the (P) role is in conflict with the (A) role?

It should have been expected that the (A) role would take "a back seat" in how the agency operated, which is what happened.

If this is what allowed the disaster to happen, if safety controls were sloppy because of this conflict of interests, then the problem is much bigger than the present leak.

Urgently, a separate government agency should be created with the exclusive role of approving and monitoring the safe operation of rigs. Who knows how many more rigs are ready to explode, too?

This structural problem within government does not end just with the Minerals Management Service. What about the FAA, which has the role to both promote aviation and control how safely it operates? And what about the Department of the Interior that manages the national parks but also grants permits to exploit the land?

In some countries the department of management and budget is within the ministry of treasury. Whose interests do they represent first, those of the government that needs money to function or of the country as a whole? It is not strange that in those countries government machinery is growing at the expense of the national economy.

In one country I have consulted for, the environmental protection agency reports to the ministry of tourism. Guess which interest is suffering more.

My forty years of management consulting have taught me that disastrous organizational architecture is the cause of many organizational disasters and this is one of them.

The Greek financial crisis

In the 1990s, when Constantine Mitsotakis was prime minister of Greece, he invited me to do a diagnosis (a "Syndag") of the country. In attendance were members of the cabinet, the president of the central bank, and leaders of the New Democracy Party, then in power.

The diagnosis revealed that the country had a mounting deficit: The government was spending more than it was collecting. How was the deficit being covered? With subsidies from the European Union. It does not take a rocket scientist to realize that subsidies will end someday. Nothing is forever.

I did not discover until later that the Greek statistical agency was presenting inaccurate economic figures that perpetuated the subsidies.

What is clear though is that the sad state of the Greek economy was a well-known secret. And no one did anything. Why? Because politicians want to get to power and stay in power; thus they are reluctant to make decisions that are not politically acceptable.

Did you know that Greek government employees get a bonus just for showing up at work? That Greek government employees retire at age 53—when most people in the world feel they are still in their prime?

How did that happen?

It is not too difficult to guess. Politicians are not statesmen. Statesmen worry about the next generation. Politicians worry about the next election.

Greek politicians were not the only ones to take the country into receivership.

This phenomenon of worrying more about the short-run goals and less, if at all, about the long-run goals, is a universal orientation, not limited to politics. Business leaders, it is claimed, focus on quarterly earnings. Marriages are not the lifetime commitment they once were. Our products are manufactured with planned obsolescence built in. Our horizon is getting closer and closer.

Greek politicians were not the only ones to take the country into receivership. Look at the state of Social Security in the United States. Or at Brazil's government expenditures as a percentage of GNP.

Maybe Greece is only the early warning of a more worrisome global phenomenon!

Economists and Reality[1]

WHEN I SUBMITTED MY DOCTORAL DISSERTATION for a Ph.D. degree at Columbia University forty-three years ago, the university ranked it as one of its top doctoral dissertations and, jointly with The Free Press, published it as a book, *Industrial Democracy Yugoslav Style* (1971).

As you might imagine, I was extremely proud.

It was years later, after I had given up my tenured professorship at UCLA and migrated into consulting, that I realized the whole dissertation was faulty. My conclusions were all wrong.

My dissertation was about the Yugoslav practice of self-management, also called "industrial democracy." I compared it to the American management theory that I had studied at school. (At that time, I had zero experience with actual practice.) My conclusion, as presented in the dissertation and subsequently in the book, was that the self-management system was deficient compared to the American system.

What was wrong with my conclusion?

I was comparing a *should* (a theory) with an *is* (a reality), instead of comparing a *should* with another *should*, or, as I did later, an *is* with another *is*.

Living in the real world

I compared apples to tomatoes—not even oranges. I compared the *theory* of one system to the *practice* of a totally different system, and obviously, practice turned out to be messier. But when I started consulting to American companies and saw how those organizations actually work, I realized that my conclusions would have been very different had I compared practice to practice.

1. Adizes Insights, October 2010.

Why am I telling you this embarrassing story?

In the *Financial Times* of August 19, 2010, Nobel Prize laureate in economics Joseph Stiglitz argued that economists don't live in the real world ("Needed: A new economic paradigm," p. 7). Because they don't, their models and theories are based on assumptions that, though they might display elegant reasoning and precise mathematical formulations, do not reflect reality.

For instance, economic theory assumes rational behavior, but in reality that just ain't so. Economic theory assumes that all actors in the market are identical, which anyone with real-life experience knows is false. It assumes perfect market functioning, in which supply and demand will balance out over time—in other words, a "hidden hand" that regulates markets. Great, Stiglitz says, except there is no hidden hand.

> *We live in an environment where problems are holistic and systemic.*

This reminds me of a joke: A physics professor, an engineer, and an economist are stranded in the desert with only one can of food and no can opener. The physics professor suggests they make a fire and place the can in it. As it expands from the heat, he explains, it will open.

"That is stupid," the engineer objects. "The can will explode, and the food will scatter. What we need is a sharp object, for leverage…"

"You are both wrong," interrupts the economist. "Let's assume we have a can opener…" (By the way I was initially trained as an economist.)

This lack of connection to reality, Stiglitz claims, is responsible for the astounding fact that not a single economic theory or model predicted the worldwide financial credit crisis. Stiglitz suggests that it is time for a new, reality-based economic theory.

Wanted: A more disciplined approach

My insight is that when economists start looking at what is really happening, as Stiglitz suggests, they are going to find out (as I did) that economic theories have insufficient tools to accurately understand reality.

We live in an environment where problems are holistic and systemic, requiring more than knowledge of economics to understand and solve them. We must also know sociology, political science, and psychology, and must free ourselves of attachment to any single theory that might interfere with objective observation—and we must use lots and lots of common sense.

If I am right, one conclusion from this insight might be that the president's Council of Economic Advisors, currently composed only of economists, should be a cross-disciplinary team, including some generalists (top executives) who know from experience how things really are, not only how they *should* be.

In general, it is prudent to beware of clean, elegant formulas based on a single theoretical discipline that limits ones capability to understand the world's messy reality.

The Invisible Hand Is Sick[1]

RECENTLY, I WAS WATCHING a well-done CNBC documentary about the causes of the credit crisis. The program included a series of interviews with people who took out subprime loans, people who sold those loans, people who securitized the loans, and the representatives of foreign entities who bought those securitized instruments.

The running theme of all these interviews was "greed." The interviewer would ask, "So, it was greed that made people do so-and-so, right?" The answer was always "yes."

Preaching greed and competition

That made me think. This greed that everyone is attacking as the cause of the breakdown, isn't it really what we preach in all our schools of business and economics? It has another name: the profit motive. Don't we teach that the more earnings per share, the better?

True, profits have to take into account the long-term needs of the organization. Very often, however, the question that must come first is how one survives in the short run.

> *The running theme of all these interviews was "greed."*

Here comes the second ingredient that we need to take into account: competition. If a certain CEO refuses to follow the short-term profit orientation, and thus his or her earnings per share are continuously inferior to what the competition is getting, he or she will be fired. Not only that, this individual will be sacrificing a significant amount of his or her personal remuneration, because a substantial part of it is almost certainly based on stock options.

1. Adizes Insights, October 2010.

So what's happening? Everyone tries to make as much profit as they can in order to be better than the competition, and in order to show successful performance.

There is an expression in the Balkans: "If you join a circle dance, you'd better dance." Similarly, if you operate in a competitive market economy where you are measured by earnings per share, you'd better gets those profits in, or you will not survive in your position.

I recognize the fact that this principle is not always universally true. The new economy, the one based on the Internet and e-commerce, can get high and growing valuations for years without making profits, as Amazon did before it moved into the black. But please notice this only happens because the investors believe that eventually the company will, in fact, make money. So the profit motive is still the driving force.

Joining the circle dance

It should be noted with that all the players in this financial credit crisis were acting legally. No one went to jail for the credit crisis. That's because no one did anything illegal. The buyers of the subprime loans believed that their equity in the house would grow. So they bought those houses assuming they would be able to refinance them later on. The salespeople selling those subprime mortgages were following their profit motive. There was a market for those mortgages: Wall Street was following its profit motive, buying those mortgages, putting them into a portfolio, rating them with a rating agency, and selling them abroad. And Wall Street was making money doing so. Any of those Wall Street companies that refused to follow the profit motive would disappear. So everyone had to join the "circle dance."

The famous "invisible hand" was working well.

The rating agencies were giving out AAA ratings because they assumed, like everyone else, that the value of homes would continue to increase; no one could predict when that upward trend would stop. If any agency had made a policy of being too conservative and refusing to pass along AAA ratings, it would have lost business to the other rating agencies and might even have disappeared from the market.

The buyers abroad were similarly motivated by the promise of profit. They bought those securitized AAA financial instruments that promised such high returns on investment, and seemed not to be too risky...because of the AAA rating.

The famous "invisible hand" was working well. (Economist Adam Smith used the phrase "invisible hand" as a metaphor for free market forces, to explain how the market regulates itself, brings growth, and secures optimal allocation of resources.)

Yet trouble was ahead. People were taking mortgages they could not afford to pay if home values ever stopped going up. That, of course, is precisely what happened. The bubble exploded, as bubbles do. Nothing is forever.

In the interview I saw, Alan Greenspan, the chairman of the Federal Reserve Board at the time, was asked, "Why did you not do anything in time to stop this potential disaster?" His response: "You think the congress would let me?"

Greenspan was right. Which politicians would dare to stand up and stop Americans from owning their home? They would be crucified by their competing politicians and would lose their offices in a hurry.

So here we have three interconnected factors: the profit motive, competition, and a political system based on promoting a popular agenda.

It is the system that is guilty

No one went to jail for the worst economic crisis we had in years. So who was at fault? All of us, and no one in particular. The system was at fault.

I repeat: No one in particular is guilty. They all individually did what they were trained to do and rewarded for doing. The system itself is the culprit, and until the system is fixed *we can expect more crises in the future.*

We have a systemic malady and it requires fixing. Singapore fixed this problem by removing one of the legs from the three-legged stool of profit motive, open competition, and political system. They do not have a competitive election system wherein political parties compete for power. One party runs the show. Party members are highly paid, and there is no corruption to speak of. Singapore has a strong government that does not cater to the electorate and does what it believes to be right.

President Barack Obama is trying to fix the problem by fixing a different leg, that of open competition. He is putting more regulation in the system, but doing so is making him politically weak. The remaining leg, the profit motive, is untouched. The new generation of young people criticize the profit motivation and would rather go surfing, but until we find another way to measure performance and reward for it, the profit motive will remain a driving force in our society.

I believe we need to redesign the system, not one leg at a time, but in its totality. The capitalist market economy and democracy as we know and experience it need reengineering. This reengineering will probably happen only after a crisis even bigger than the one we just experienced. Unfortunately, such a crisis seems inevitable.

Why "Let the Consumer Beware" Does Not Work in Practice[1]

BUSINESS ORGANIZATIONS, when challenged, often defend their questionable practices by saying: "Let the consumer beware."

For example, that is how the tobacco companies defend marketing their cigarettes, which, as we all know, cause cancer to those smoking them as well as those who inhale them secondhand. The tobacco companies claim to believe that the customer should be able to choose whether to smoke or not. Free country, right?

And how about TV programs that depict violence, casual sex, or vulgar behavior? Consumers are free to change the channel, right?

The myth of free choice

What about food that can cause obesity, hardening of the arteries, maybe even cancer? Again: Let the consumer decide. People have a choice. Free country. Free choice.

But are we really free to choose?

The free-choice argument assumes that we, the consumers, are in control of our actions, our choices. It assumes that we can make the choice. But to be able to choose freely, we must be well informed about what repercussions our choices will have.

A lot has been done toward informing consumers about the ingredients in their packaged food. There is even a trend in restaurants to tell patrons what goes into the food they are ordering. But this makes the assumption that the data given to consumers is "information." What is the definition of information? Information is data that is organized in such a way that it can aid decision making.

1. Adizes Insights, January 2011.

Unfortunately, in reality, most food packaging gives you data, not information. For instance, manufacturers can, and do, hide the fact that their product contains lots of sugar by calling it something else. It takes a food engineer or nutrition expert to understand what it says on the food package.

But let us give the food companies the benefit of the doubt and assume that their packaging offers us usable information, from which we can learn the dangers of consuming the product.

What about TV programs? Is it enough just to warn the viewer about potentially offensive content? Would you call such a warning *data*, or is it *information*? To be information, it needs to remind us of the repercussions of watching the program; in other words, what will it do to us? If it does not remind us of the *repercussions*, it is not effective as a warning. In fact, because what is forbidden attracts, the warning could have the opposite effect, tempting us even more strongly to watch the program.

Knowing is not enough

But, again, even though I doubt it, let us assume we understand the repercussions of the choices we make. Is that all we need in order to be in control of our actions?

I suggest that knowing is not enough. We must also have the willpower to act on what we know. Do we always have that willpower? I suggest that we do not, because of something called "addiction."

Many people have an addiction to cigarettes. To alcohol. To violence on TV. (Yes, that's right: addiction to violence.) To sex. To certain foods. The common denominator to all these addictions is pleasure—and the more pleasure they give, and the faster they give that pleasure, the more addictive they are going to be.

Pushing pleasure

The food industry, alcohol, and TV programming are all "pleasure pushers." They work hard to please us as much and as fast as they can. This is called "good business," because it is extremely profitable. But it also causes us to become addicted.

Mottos such as "Let the customer beware," and "The customer has a choice," are mere fig leaves to disguise strategies that foster addiction. As a result, businesses are able to make profits even if their products cause disease, mental health problems, and social disintegration.

What to do?

In making social policy, we have a choice: Should we prohibit dysfunctional, addiction-causing products and services (and if we do, then we should prohibit them across the board, not just selectively depending on how powerful a lobby it has); or should we allow market forces to provide those addictive products and services, and let the customer beware?

I suggest that knowing is not enough.

Both choices have their benefits, but also their costs.

The "freedom to choose," it should be understood, has costs: the current obesity epidemic in the United States, crimes that mimic those on TV programs, deaths caused by drunken drivers.

On the other hand, when Prohibition (of alcohol) was attempted in the US, it did not work. People found ways to produce and consume it despite the law.

Nevertheless, I would still choose prohibition (and, in the case of television, censorship) because, in my judgment, the price we are paying for our "freedom" is much higher than the price of giving up a phony "freedom" that is rendered useless by addiction anyway.

The Global, Economic, Financial Crisis[1]

I AM IN MOSCOW, watching the BBC. There is a live roundtable discussion with very prominent economists as to what the USA and Europe should do about the global financial and economic crisis. Their concerns: unemployment, declining economic growth, recession, potential for country defaults, etc.

Around the table are the managing director of the International Monetary Fund; the CEO of Pimco, a global investment firm; a distinguished professor of economics from Chicago; and another person with a heavy Italian accent whose name I failed to record.

To summarize what they are saying, there is a crisis of unemployment, the financial markets are sick, and there is declining economic growth. The result: a serious crisis with potential for a double-dip recession, and potential for a default by some countries. They recommend different solutions how to solve the financial crisis, how to improve the rate of employment, etc.

A final solution

The common denominator to their solutions is that they are trying to get back to what we had before, which is full employment, healthy financial markets, and economic growth.

It will not work.

If we succeed in going back, it will be only a temporary solution and the crisis will return as a tsunami, much bigger, later on.

Why?

Let us analyze the problem. Economic growth, unemployment, financial

1. Adizes Insights, November 2011.

crisis, double-dip recession, and dangers of default are not of equal nature. My analysis is that the driving force is economic growth, which provides for full employment and for which healthy financial markets are necessary. That means that economic growth is the goal, and full employment and healthy financial markets are the means. Double-dip recession and dangers of default are manifestations of lack of economic growth.

The problem is with the goal. And from there stem the problems with the means.

What is the problem with the goal of economic growth? (My focus here is exclusively on developed nations. What to do with emerging, developing nations will be addressed at the end of this insight.)

In order to have economic growth, we need to have growing markets.

How do you have growing markets? One way is to have a growing population. That apparently is not enough. Businesses create markets by creating needs—needs markets did not know they had. Look at the choices offered to consumers on any product in a supermarket. Or a department store. Furthermore, to create markets, to create demand, products are produced with planned obsolescence in mind.

In order to have economic growth, we need to have growing markets.

But what is the result of having continuously growing markets as a goal? It is not sustainable. If we paraphrase Thomas Malthus and instead of population growth say "economic growth," and instead of food production say "natural resources," we can see that linear progression of economic growth must eventually bring us to a point where there are limits to growth: We are destroying the planet.

A new way of thinking

So the solution to the financial, economic, unemployment crisis is not more of what used to be, more economic growth. We need something new. A paradigm shift in our thinking.

Economic growth should not be our deterministic goal, a goal where more is better, a goal we are determined to maximize. Economic growth should now become a constraint goal: no less than x%, when x is determined by population growth and real needs, not by artificial needs generation.

What should be the deterministic goal then, if it is not economic growth? Quality of life rather than the standard of living. Who says we should have full employment? Why not have very early retirement? Why not have only three working days in a week? Earn enough to satisfy your basic needs. Not more and more and more. Just enough.

But a decimated demand and planned unemployment will dry up the need for credit and for business growth and put the financial institutions in trouble.

I sure hope so.

The solution to our present problems is not going back to our past but creating a new future.

Now, what about developing, emerging, nations? For emerging ones—and especially those unfortunate to suffer from malnutrition, from lack of health treatment facilities, etc.—the need for economic growth is real.

There, the goal should be economic growth, but please notice: It is not going back for them. It is going forward. They need economic growth. They never had it. Here the business community of the developed world should do its best to develop the market, satisfy the needs of the population.

"But there is no market there, no buying power," will be the excuse. That is the *true* challenge to the business community. Not the artificial, self-created challenge of how to provide more of something people have too much of already.

THE FORTHCOMING CRISIS[1]

I JUST FINISHED PARTICIPATING in a webinar organized by Humanity's Team, the group that hosted Global Oneness Day. There was a very stimulating discussion about the future of humanity. I want to share with you what I said and what I think.

In one of my previous blog posts, I wrote that capitalism was dying in front of our eyes. In light of what I learned in this broadcast, I want to rephrase the title of that essay.

The real culprit: The stock market

Capitalism is not dying. It is flourishing. It is taking over the world. What is dying is the capitalist model. It does not work anymore. It brought us an unparalleled standard of living, but it is destroying our quality of life. It is destroying the planet, which we all share.

What is wrong?

The fault lies with the very foundation of capitalism, its capital markets. And the foundation of capital markets is the stock market. Yes, the stock market. What is wrong with it? It de facto bifurcates owners from the companies they supposedly own.

Capitalism is not dying. It is flourishing.

Let me explain. Owners of shares move from one company to another in a heartbeat. Should another company offer higher returns on investment, stockholders are quick to shift their holdings. Their behavior is not that of real owners. They are speculators.

What about the board of directors? Do not they represent the owners? Yes,

1. Adizes Insights, October 2012.

but how? By maximizing profits that the company generates. If the CEO does not produce profits that are better or comparable to other companies in the industry, he or she will be replaced quickly.

So profits, return on investment, and earnings per share are what drive companies' management, boards of directors, and the so-called owners.

As every company tries to maximize its profits, the planet is being destroyed. The total system is sub-optimized as the corporate world pursues a policy of each one for himself to his own individual benefit.

That no longer works today. The world is too interdependent. Our resources are fixed. As we consume more, the planet is becoming depleted.

It starts with business education

Who is at fault? I believe that our business schools within academia are one of the main culprits. They are training thousands, if not millions, of today's business leaders around the world. Their credo is a straightforward one: The future lies in the hands of corporate leaders who can design the best business models geared to maximizing profits.

What can we do? First, we need to change business education. Then, we need to change our economic theory, which bases itself exclusively on mathematical value-free models. And, finally, we need to train future and present leaders to be professionals who understand the importance of limits. Who recognize that limits are driven by values, not by numbers.

Take medical schools. What are medical doctors trained to do? To follow the Hippocratic oath: "do no harm." A medical doctor can maximize profits by prescribing unnecessary surgeries, unnecessary repetitive visits. But a professional, "do no harm" doctor will focus on the health of patients rather than on profits.

Which means profits should not be a deterministic goal to be maximized, but a constraint goal not to be violated.

Profit is a boundary. Not a goal. A professional doctor does not want to be bankrupt. However, his focus should be the welfare of the patient.

In the case of the business world, the goal needs to be one of adding value albeit profitably. Thus, to maximize profits, stop selling and promoting food that is full of sugar, food that is processed to the point of spreading obesity, diabetes, and high blood pressure. Stop polluting the air, water, and the earth we live on.

Changing behavior

Reorganize the financial markets that have only one concern: return on investment. Replace the stock market with the bond market. Let the people who work in the company own the company. Have representatives of the public, not only the owners, sit on the board of directors. Have socially conscious people like artists sit on the boards.

If we want to change behavior, we need to change the power structure of organizations.

> *The world is marching over the cliff to a disaster.*

Organizations are like motor boats. If one engine is very strong, and the other very weak, no matter how much shouting you do on the deck, the direction the boat will take is predictable.

Profit-oriented institutions are too strong today. They have capital markets. They have schools for training future leaders. They have measurements to monitor success; a reward structure geared to maximize profits. And they unite themselves into strategic alliances. They use the most sophisticated psychological models to brainwash customers to buy products they do not even know they need.

Arrayed against them are socially conscious organizations, which are weak, not united, fighting among themselves for donations. With only sporadic leadership training and no significant alliances. Without research. Without development. Armed only with good intentions. Good luck.

A systemic disaster

The world is marching over the cliff to a disaster. How the engines are aligned is driving the planet boat to a disaster. A disaster that will be pale in comparison to 1929, which was an economic disaster. The calamities we are experiencing at present and increasingly in the future are not just economic. Or just social. They are systemic.

Our world today, and increasingly so tomorrow, is far too complex and interdependent. For instance, a technological change has almost instantaneous social, cultural, and economic repercussions. In other words, we live in a more complex world than 1929 and our problems are, and will be, systemic in nature. Very complex and very global.

Whoever gets elected to be the president of United States in 2012 will have bigger and more acute problems than the president who was elected in 2008.

And whoever is elected in 2012 will wish he had the problems of 2008. The problems are getting bigger. More complex. More systemic. And who might take over to solve them? Big government. Who else? We have already been conditioned to dependency. Our government is responsible for taking care of us. We are marching towards a new middle ages, a new feudal age, governed not by monarchy or the church but by bureaucrats and bureaucracy.

Who will solve the problem?

Big government will not solve the problems. It will accentuate them. And hide them by suppressing rights and freedoms. Why? Because bureaucracies by definition are control freaks.

Unless we unite now to deal with the problems, that is our future.

How do we unite? There are about a billion people who support NGOs. Just imagine if they got together, truly together, to follow a plan of action. To meet goals that they jointly support. Instead of one organization protecting the whales, another the dolphins, and a third the gorillas.... Imagine if all together they selected one item at a time and worked to pass legislation that would help us all. For instance, repeal the law that it is a punishable offense not to maximize profits. (Do you know that in the US stockholders can sue boards and management if they can prove that management did not try to maximize profits?) Delegitimize business schools that teach that profits are the goal of corporations. Delegitimize Milton Friedman's theoretical framework that corporations exist for their shareholders only, and profit is the exclusive measurement of their interests.

Will it happen? Unfortunately it calls for a paradigm change. A change in thinking. A major change in values.

Paradigms change with a crisis, and for a major paradigm shift we need a major crisis.

It is coming. But if we do not prepare for it the solution might be worse than the problem: an unmanageable bureaucracy.

CRISIS, INNOVATION, AND ENTREPRENEURSHIP[1]

The above title was the subject of a regional convention held in Podgorica, Montenegro, on September 20, 2013. It was opened by the first Deputy Prime Minister, after which I was asked to deliver a short presentation. I do not have the transcript. Here is what I said from memory.

CRISIS COMES FROM THE GREEK LANGUAGE, and it means—I find this interesting—that it is time to do something different. In Hebrew the word for crisis is *mashber*, which comes from the root "something broke up." The same is true for the meaning of the word in Chinese.

There is a common denominator here: Crisis means that whatever we have had until now does not work anymore, and it is time to do something else, and to do it differently.

> *Innovation, by definition, means doing something different, something new.*

Innovation, by definition, means doing something different, something new. Therefore, crisis provides a perfect environment for innovation. It offers us a chance to come up with fresh and different ways to satisfy an old or new need.

However, it should be stressed, not all innovations are successful. Quite the contrary. Most fail. To be effective, to succeed, innovations need an entrepreneur who will invest time, energy, and money to make the new ideas and approach commercially acceptable.

The need for an entrepreneur

That brings us to the next important question: What are the conditions for successful entrepreneurship? In other words, what does an entrepreneur need if he is determined to introduce innovation?

First, a caveat: Whenever we introduce innovation and wish to make it

1. Adizes Insights, October 2013.

successful, we have to deal with uncertainty and risk. They are not one and the same thing. Uncertainty deals with insufficient information. Innovation, by definition, cannot give us historical data on which to base our judgment. And the future, of course, is unknown. Thus, uncertainty.

Risk is different. To commercialize or just monetize an innovation we need to provide energy, time, and resources. All three are necessary if we wish to succeed. There is always a chance our efforts to innovate might not work, and our time, energy, and resources will be wasted. That is the risk.

Entrepreneurs of course want to have as little uncertainty as possible, and controllable risk as well. In a time of crisis, however, uncertainty is high, as is risk. That might tend to discourage entrepreneurs from embarking on a new path, from trying to innovate. They might want to wait until the dust settles. But waiting might not be the right strategy. They might lose the window of opportunity and someone else might step in and seize the chance to innovate.

What to do?

In my opinion, here is where government has a role to play. As long as potential entrepreneurs trust the government, trust the leaders, there is hope. And when there is hope, uncertainty and risk are not quite as threatening. It is trust in the system in which the entrepreneurs operate that makes uncertainty and risk tolerable. It is the absence of hope, and of trust, that is damaging.

In this time of financial crisis, in my work as a consultant to national governments, I have been asked by several prime ministers and presidents for advice. They expected an answer composed of some sophisticated economic policy or of some elaborate financial strategy. My answer to all of them was the same: "Whatever you do, do not lose the trust of the people."

For example, look at the recent crisis in Cyprus and the way the government handled it. Their solution was to freeze people's bank accounts. What did that do to trust? Depositors will not deposit in Cyprus again, not for a long, long time. It was a short tactical solution with enormous long-term strategic repercussions. Cyprus will never be the safe harbor for foreign investors that it used to be.

How about devaluation of the currency? Again, when people lose trust in money, what happens? Always be careful with how much money you print and flood into the market in order to ease a credit crunch. Inflation has a serious impact on trust.

Crisis can be an opportunity to change, to innovate, to encourage entrepreneurship, to improve the system, and flourish again, but only as long as trust is not hurt.

THE ECONOMIC
GROWTH CHALLENGE [1]

I AM READING A BOOK, *The Great Degeneration*[2], by a prominent Harvard professor. In it, he analyzes the decline of the West as measured by economic growth. Our economies are stagnating, he claims.

More is not always better

I have no disagreement with his facts. I am, however, uncomfortable with his conclusions. His starting point is that economic stagnation is a bad thing. I disagree. More is not always better. It depends where you are on the Life-cycle. For a start-up company, just as for a growing child, or for an emerging economy, more *is* better. No question.

But for a company in post-Go-Go, or for a grown person, or for a nation with what I would call a "saturated economy," more is not always "more." It often ends up being less. There is more in one thing but less in something else. On the margin, what we gain in one field is much less than what we lose on the other field.

What am I referring to?

I have noticed that in developed economies the standard of living keeps rising while the quality of life goes down. Men and women are chasing after more and more economic wellness, but have less and less time to enjoy what they already have. We have more possessions but with more stress. I witness more laughter in one day in developing countries than in a whole year in a developed country.

If we place quality of life on the vertical axis and economic growth on the horizontal axis, the curve that shows the relation of the two variables will be,

1. Adizes Insights, June 2014.

2. N. Ferguson. The Great Degeneration: How Institutions Decay and Economies Die. New York: Penguin Press HC, 2013.

say, a normal distribution. It will not be linear, ascending up and up forever.

A "saturated economy" to me is one where, on the margins, one more unit of economic wellness produces one less unit of quality of life. Do we need in America one hundred different versions of bread? And indeed the enormous choices in almost everything? And planned obsolescence? What a tremendous cost we pay for this abundance in human energy to produce and distribute it.

Emerging economies need more of what they already have because they have so little. But why us? Economic stagnation, a halt to chasing growth as if it were a necessity, is exactly what we need.

What should be our new goal then? Improving our quality of life.

Years ago while I was driving along the coast from San Diego, California to Los Angeles, and as I was gazing out the window, I had an insight about the past and the possible future of civilization. First I saw agricultural fields. Then there were chimneys. Then I reached Laguna Beach, a small picturesque town populated mainly by artists, many of whom live quite modestly, enjoying their leisure time.

This is it, I said to myself. This is the future. This is how it should be: Take early retirement. When you are young, earn enough for food and shelter to feel secure in old age, and when you reach your saturation point, stop working for more money. That is when you should start working to secure free time to grow emotionally, socially, and artistically.

> *Current strategic theory tells us that if we do not grow we die.*

Once I had a client who challenged consultants and economic theory. He said to me that he disagreed with consultants who constantly preach growth, and who tell him that he needs to grow more. He is happy to be a hundred-million-dollar company forever, he said. It is good enough for him because he wants to enjoy his life, his free time and his family.

Current strategic theory tells us that if we do not grow we die. Not true. We need to change, yes, but change does not necessarily mean to grow.

A company needs to change. Granted, it needs to adapt to a changing environment. If it does not do so it becomes irrelevant and will be abandoned by its customers and die.

Okay, but change does not necessarily mean growth in quantity. It can mean growth in quality. "Bigger is not necessarily better." "Better can be more, but in quality of life....."

It is possible for a person or family to say "We have enough. Now let us enjoy what we have." The same can apply to a company that can decide that its present size meets its needs, and it will now focus on striving continuously to be the best it can be at its present scale. For that, it will constantly change and improve on what it does, how and why.

But this idea or principle does not apply only to people or companies. It can apply to society as well.

The nation can concentrate on "better" national quality of life: freer time, more art, culture, sports, mental and physical health improvement, less crime, less mental disease, better education. There is so much more to life than how much we have not only for a person, family or a company, but for the nation as well.

Take unemployment. One way to solve it, of course, is to have more economic activity. So we are back into "more is better." But what if we change our goals, so that we emphasize the importance and necessity of maintaining a higher quality of life? How then might we solve unemployment?

Have job sharing. Then the weekend for people will consist of three or four days rather than only two. Play more. Work less. More people will work but less. But then people will earn less money, you might reasonably say. That is exactly the idea. It is not necessary to have more. Just enough.

Why does the US have to be the economic powerhouse of the world? Why can it not be a country with the best quality of life, complete with art, sports, and time and space for self-growth?

Post-industrial society should not stand for more economic growth. We need to change goals as we move up the lifecycle curve. Not only in personal and corporate life, but also in national policy.

PART V

GLOBAL CHALLENGES IN LEADING CHANGE

Is the Cordoba Initiative's Islamic Center for Ground Zero for Real?[1]

IF IMAM FEISAL ABDUL RAUF and his financial backers truly want to build a Muslim center that promotes moderation, they need to walk their talk. And if they do, I believe the Islamic Community Center—even at Ground Zero itself, not just close by—is most appropriate.

A list of suggestions

If those who support the Cordoba Initiative want to promote non-radical behavior, why don't they dedicate one or two floors in the center to a permanent exhibit denouncing the atrocities that radical Muslims have committed in the last fifteen years?

How about a film showing Muslim women being stoned to death for the alleged crime of adultery by those radicals they denounce? Show exhibits of the bombings in London and Madrid. Show the scattered body parts. And, of course, do not skip the terror attacks in Israel, which killed even small children in their nurseries.

I would like to see a room dedicated to beheadings, especially of Daniel Pearl, who was beheaded in front of video cameras, only—I repeat, only—because he was a Jew. Show the whole tape, non-stop. Let the audience squirm. Let children scream in disgust.

What about dedicating one floor to the September 11 terror attacks? Tell the whole world about the Muslims who piloted those planes meant to kill innocent people. Tell visitors where the terrorists got their religious education, and who paid for it.

Develop educational programs for Muslim children, so that they too will be disgusted and learn to denounce Muslim terrorism.

1. Adizes Insights, October 2010.

The Germans denounced the Nazis. About two years ago, during a trip to Berlin, I visited the Holocaust Museum, near the Brandenburg Gate in the heart of the city, spitting distance from Hitler's bunker. With this museum the German people were openly washing their dirty linen. By exhibiting pictures of atrocities committed during the Holocaust, they were denouncing the Nazis' crimes loud and clear.

If the founders of the Muslim center really denounce radical Islam, let them prove it in action not just words.

If the founders of the Muslim center really denounce radical Islam, let them prove it in action not just words.

I have met Imam Rauf, and I believe he is a sincere, well-meaning leader of the Muslim religion. But even though he is here today, sometime in the future he will be gone. Nobody is immortal. Having this permanent exhibit will assure us that this center, located on hallowed ground, does not become another hub of radical Muslim activity, applauding September 11 rather than denouncing it, after he departs the scene. If the center ever took down the exhibits, we would know its leader's goals had changed.

Another point of importance: This exhibit will test the real intentions of the financial backers of the center. If the commitment to the exhibit causes them to disappear, along with their funds, maybe some of the people who are supporting the center financially are the same people who finance the madrassas that glorify jihad and suicide terrorism.

If the Imam wants our trust, he must denounce radical Islam, not only in words, but in deeds.

Author's Note: This essay was sent to the op ed pages of the New York Times, *the* Washington Post, *the* Los Angeles Times, *and the* Wall Street Journal, *who all rejected it. The* Santa Barbara News-Press *published it October 3, 2010.*

THE MUSLIM THREAT?[1]

THE WESTERN WORLD has developed a serious case of Islamophobia. The reasons are obvious: Terrorist attacks by radical Muslims have become a regular occurrence; added to that, Western Europe is starting to grasp the possibility that, because of immigration and the high birthrate among Muslims, Europe's population will soon have a Muslim majority.

Is this fear justifiable?

Identifying the problem

I suggest that it is not necessarily so. Not all Muslims are now, or even potentially, the "enemy." I, for instance, owe my life to a family of Albanian Muslims, who hid and sheltered me and my parents during World War II.

There *are* peace-loving Muslims, with strong family values and high morals.

The Taliban are not the first or only zealots.

So, what, exactly, is the problem?

My insight is that we are not engaged in a religious war, or a cultural war. This isn't about Muslims against Judeo-Christians. This is an ageless struggle between those who support and nourish diversity, and those who believe in only one right way to do *everything*—whether it is politics, religion, or sex—and would like to outlaw or eliminate every other alternative.

This was the source of the conflict between Sparta and Athens in the fifth century B.C. Fifteen centuries later, the same conflict drove both twentieth-century world wars: The allied nations on one side believed democracy was the least flawed form of government, while those on the opposing side wanted a single-party system, enforced by a totalitarian regime.

1. Adizes Insights, July 2011.

The Taliban are not the first or only zealots. Think about the Spanish Inquisition in the fifteenth century. Weren't the Inquisitors a Christian version of the Taliban? The only difference is that now it's 500 years later, and the zealots are Muslim.

Every religion attracts a certain number of fanatics, people who focus obsessively on promoting and defending their *own* rules while prosecuting or purging anyone whose beliefs happen to differ. In their view, persecuting these "others" is not only virtuous, but obligatory.

Fanatical belief systems inevitably reach a point at which terrorism seems like a logical next step. So they terrorize: burning down other people's houses of prayer.

What to do?

Bring everyone inside the circle

Wars won't fix this; you cannot effectively fight hate with hate. I believe I have figured out how democratic forces can win this war.

Here is my insight: The way to prevail against those who believe in one and *only* one way, is to use their own belief system against them.

How?

Think of a society or culture as a large, amorphous, encompassing shape. When you exclude everybody who is unlike you, you create a boundary line, a circle. Now, everyone *inside* the circle is one of the faithful, and those *outside* the circle are infidels, to be handled in whatever ways are deemed useful, or simply eliminated.

But this circle is not fixed. It is dynamic. Those inside the circle now look for who does not fit inside the circle too. Their need is to sameness. The need for no diversity has to be directed now at the people inside the circle because outside the circle have been excluded already.

For example, look at some Jewish religious fanatics. First, they excluded the *goyim*, i.e., anyone not born to a Jewish mother. Then they excluded Jews who pray with a different intonation, such as the Sephardim. Then they even started to exclude each other based on how each interprets the Torah. And within each small sub-cult, there began to be more exclusions. The circle just keeps shrinking.

Instead of fighting exclusionists, we ought to isolate them and hermetically seal their borders. Without a convenient "enemy" population on which to concentrate their blame and fear, they will soon start arguing among them-selves: "Who is the most religious? Who is the most faithful?" It will end in violence, as usual, but this time they will be fighting and killing each other, and their society will collapse in on itself, as all rotten things eventually do.

> *The way to prevail against those who believe in one and only one way, is to use their own belief system.*

Meanwhile, the media—radio, TV, Internet, books—which do not recognize borders, can be used by democratic forces to speed up their disintegration process. In addition, democratic forces can offer financial aid to those inside these countries who support democracy.

But it is equally essential that pro-diversity countries protect their diversity. They must enact strict laws that outlaw any and all efforts to foster non-diversity.

This is a war between different philosophies, different outlooks on life. It is a war of styles, not of religions.

What Is Wrong with "Occupy Wall Street" Demonstrations[1]

L ET ME START WITH THE BOTTOM LINE, with my conclusion: They are demonstrating in the wrong place against the wrong people.

Now, let me explain.

Most of the demonstrations have placards about greed, about how Wall Street companies and executives earn obscene sums of money while the rest of the country is truly suffering. American companies are awash in record profits while unemployment is at record highs. Something is genuinely not right… But what they are demonstrating against are the manifestations of the problem not the cause of the problem.

Locating the cause of the problem

What is the cause? The profit motive. That is where the problem is.

Imagine what would happen if medical doctors turned profit oriented and measured their success by profits. If medical schools taught them that profit should be the goal by which they should measure their success. Many of us would die from unnecessary surgeries, go bankrupt from never-ending medical bills or insurance premiums, and productivity of labor would go way, way down because we would be hospitalized to no end.

What does medical training say? "Do no harm! The patient is first!"

Doctors need to get paid, but it is not the pay that should drive their decision making. I emphasized the word "should" because, in reality, some doctors do succumb to the pressures of society to measure themselves by how much they earn, and have compromised their professional judgment for the sake of making money. But they are the anomaly, not the norm; whereas in business, it is the declared, legitimate, sought-after norm.

1. Adizes Insights, October 2011.

Look how the pharmaceutical companies behave. To get repetitive, sustainable, profits, they supposedly develop new drugs. In reality, they are doing continuous improvement to old drugs and calling them new drugs to justify their R&D expenses. They discover new diseases that need treatment, although there is doubt about their severity.

Pharmaceutical companies are making tons of money while the country is going bankrupt as health care expenses are getting out of hand. Are they really patient oriented, or do they see the patients as a source of opportunities to make money?

The profit motive. That is where the problem is.

What I am describing here is happening not only within the health care industry, it is happening with the whole business world. Each CEO is trying to make better earnings per share, especially if the company is in the stock market. If his earnings per share are below those of the competition the CEO will be replaced.

There is no shame in focusing on profits. That is what business schools teach and what schools of economics justify with endless logical mathematical proofs. To increase profits and have them grow sustainably, companies invent goods and services, whose social justification is marginal at best, and penetrate new markets, where the benefits to the new market are questionable. We know, for instance, that soft drinks are full of sugar, causing obesity and heart attacks. Still, we export them worldwide. Fried food also causes obesity, high blood pressure, and a myriad of other diseases. Poor people use fast food as their nourishment; they have no money to buy healthier foods, or do not know better. Los Angeles' local government has forbidden opening fast food outlets in poor parts of the city. But we nevertheless export those same products to any poor country we can and destroy their health. And make money.

The whole system is profit oriented to the detriment of the market it serves.

I am not pointing a finger at the CEOs, by the way. Individually, they are conscious, spiritual people, or at least some of them are. It is the system of rewards and punishment that causes them to behave a certain way.

Serving the client

What to do? Business leaders should be professionals, like MDs. Put the client first. Do no harm.

Instead of profit being the goal, it should be the limitation. In other words, serving the clients profitably should be the goal, rather than increasing profitability and letting the customers beware. Assertions that "consumers are grown up...information is available...free choice, etc." I consider fig leaves to cover greed.

A change in focus

So, where should the demonstrators demonstrate? In front of the business schools and schools of economics where they indoctrinate business leaders, where the legitimization of profits is done.

> *When a person knows he is facing certain death, the real truth of what life is about comes out.*

The profit motive is deeply ingrained in our education. One reason for this is that profit provides a goal that can be quantified. Quantification of goals enables professors to develop beautiful mathematical models and theories, which they would not be able to do otherwise. Client orientation, professional treatment of clients, and not doing harm are not easily quantifiable. With the profit measurement big corporations, especially multinationals, can be controlled. There is a measurable criterion of success or failure. With non-quantifiable criteria, like professionalism and client care, such controls could not be as accurate.

We have developed a whole ideology of business that would rather be precisely wrong than approximately right.

The ideal executive: Steve Jobs not Jack Welch

My hero is not Jack Welch of General Electric, the "burn and slice" executive who made ROI the idol to worship. My hero is Steve Jobs, who loved his clients, his application developers, and his computer developments. And the customers loved him in return, as did the developers and the employees; people fought to get hired by Apple.

Do you think that Steve Jobs could have developed Apple into the most valuable company on earth if he was just profit motivated? Profit was the result of the love he had for everything he did. He said, "Remembering that you are going to die is the best way I know to avoid the trap of thinking you have something to lose. You are already naked. There is no reason not to follow your heart."

Did he say anything about making as much money as you can before dying? He followed his heart. Our business education has nothing about following the heart. All business courses are about how to make more and better money. I know: I taught in several business schools.

When a person knows he is facing certain death, the real truth of what life is about comes out. And it is love. Love for whatever we do.

I, and I bet you too, will go to a doctor who loves his profession more than he loves his wallet. And I want to train and develop managers and executives who love what they do for their customers (however profitably) more than how much profit they have made.

My conclusion is that the Occupy demonstrators are protesting the leaves of the tree, not its roots. Because they apparently do not see the roots. They demonstrate against what they see. I wish they would demonstrate in front of Harvard Business School, the Kremlin of business education, the school that trained those who are being demonstrated against. Demonstrate in front of the Chicago School of Economics, where Milton Friedman got a Nobel Prize for religiously defending that the purpose of business is business.

They are the culprits. We are the victims.

IS IT A WAR ON TERRORISM OR SOMETHING ELSE?[1]

A FRIEND SENT ME A LINK to a YouTube video showing Muslims burning the American flag in front of the American Embassy in London this year on September 11. As I watched the video, I became upset. How dare they burn the American flag, and how dare they choose that sacred day on which to do it?

But then I listened to a demonstrator, dressed in typical Muslim garb, as he spoke through a loudspeaker with a perfect Oxford English accent. "Hello Britain, America!" he said. "How many of your children have to die for you to realize this is a religious war? A war *you* are waging against us."

A different language

Wait! *We* are waging war against *them*? Are we not *defending* ourselves from them?

Let us go over his message carefully in the spirit of mutual respect.

Please note: I do not in any way support or condone what Muslim terrorists did on September 11, or any other act of terrorism. But the demonstrator's remark made me think: If we reframe our democracy, our laws, and our justice system as "*our* sharia" in contrast to their totalitarian religious practice and their religious laws—*their* sharia—then their accusation that we are trying to impose our sharia upon them makes sense.

We *are*. We object to how they treat their women. But put yourself in their shoes: How do you think *they* feel about how we treat *our* women? They see our women dressed seductively in public. They see that our women are frequently divorced or unmarried, and that most people in this country think abortion is morally okay. Why would they want to adopt our way of life?

1. Adizes Insights, November 2011.

We do not want their women to come to school with a head scarf covering their hair, although Muslim women wear the hijab not only for modesty but also because it allows them to be judged by their morals, character, and ideals instead of their appearance. Our women come to school in clothes that reveal their legs, their arms, and often their cleavage. In our culture, that is normal, but in their society, only promiscuous women—whores—dress and behave like that. They do not want to see their daughters or wives become Western in dress or behavior.

What we call freedom of choice may well look to them like brazen contempt toward the social values they hold sacred. Why would they embrace "our sharia" any more enthusiastically than we are willing to embrace *their* sharia?

We object to how they treat their women.

We object to them trying to bring their sharia laws into our country, but we think it is legitimate to go to their country and by force impose "our sharia" on them. Granted, it is appropriate to take action to prevent our enemies from developing weapons of mass destruction or conspiring to attack us in any other way. But is that the reason we are *still* in Iraq? Afghanistan?

Using the wrong tools

We believe their values are from the Stone Age. But do we have the right to use force to change their values?

We are using the wrong tools to bring our sharia to them: Arms. Mortar. Bombing. Killing. None of which change minds. Only a mind can change a mind. Did the Arab Spring, toppling dictators, happen by us invading Egypt with our tanks and army, or did it happen through exposure to mass media—our mass media? Did the Berlin Wall fall because we invaded Russia or was it the result of our TV programs being watched across the Wall, creating expectations for change, changing minds and thus behavior?

Today's wars are not conducted with rifles, or machine guns. They are conducted with small, easy-to-carry video cameras, and broadcast via YouTube and Facebook.

It takes two to tango and if we believe it is right and moral to change their sharia to ours, fighting to do it might be aggravating the problem rather than solving it.

Montesquieu and Democracy[1]

IT IS THE INFLUENCE of the French philosopher Montesquieu that led to the separation of powers necessary for democracy as a system of governance. These three powers, or branches, are the executive, the legislative, and the judicial.

In my opinion, what Montesquieu preached was right, but incomplete. Why?

All about roles

Let us analyze it using the PAEI code.

I suggest to you that the legislative branch performs the (E) role. I imagine you will disagree and claim that it is the (A) role; however, I suggest that the results of its work are (A), but its real purpose is (E). The purpose of legislation is to direct the country, to make decisions that determine what the country will do or look like. That is the (E) role.

The role of the executive branch is (P): to execute decisions of the legislative branch, and/or to recommend legislation to them.

What about the judicial branch? Here I see the (A) role. This branch interprets and enforces the law. That is why they are very concerned with following precedents.

Even if you disagree with my classification of the branches of democratic government in PAEI terms, you must agree that what is missing is the (I) role, an (I) branch. This is a shame considering how badly it is needed in light of the rate of change we are experiencing in modern life.

This (I) exists in certain forms of governments such as presidential democracies and monarchies. The president or monarch is above all the political

1. Adizes Insights, December 2011.

struggles. He or she is not a member of any of the three branches, but is instead the single person above them all.

Why do we need this (I) role in the form of a higher entity? To keep the unity of the country by symbolizing it. Otherwise the political fights for power and the struggle between the branches reduce the trust the population has in its governing institutions. Someone has to symbolize the unity of the country, nourish it, and protect it.

Unfortunately in the United States the president is a member of the executive branch. If he tries to unify the country he is considered a non-leader, because he is not taking a position. Yet if he takes a position he is too divisive.

This is not strange at all because the (P) and (I) roles are incompatible.

Food for thought.

THE CAUSES OF TRUST AND ITS IMPLICATIONS[1]

I THINK I HAVE DISCOVERED the source of respect. It is embedded in the belief that you can benefit from the person disagreeing with you, that there is something to be learned from the disagreement. As if saying: "I will respect your disagreement so long as I believe I can learn from it... and so long as you disagree without becoming disagreeable."

What makes some people trust while others react with suspicion?

Respect is earned mostly with—and learned from—experience. The utmost respect occurs when you believe that you can learn from everyone without the need for proof. When your personality is open and curious all the time, you grant respect to everyone.

But what about trust? What makes some people trust while others react with suspicion?

A question of belief

I think I found an answer. It depends on whether you believe in a growing or in a fixed, or worse, in a shrinking pie.

Let me explain.

A belief in a growing pie is the belief that in the future things will be better. There will be more for all of us. So whoever works hard and contributes to the pie will only make it grow (which will benefit everyone). And for that reason we will not object too much if he or she is exceptionally rewarded.

A belief in a fixed pie is a belief that what is available is limited, so if some-

1. Adizes Insights, February 2014.

one works hard, it does not mean the pie will grow. On the contrary, if he works extremely hard and by doing so manages to secure a bigger piece of the pie, there will be less for us. Thus, people try to undermine the ambitious worker and make it difficult for him to excel and in doing so prevent him from taking a larger share of the pie.

In a society with a shrinking-pie belief system, there is an attempt even to delegitimize anyone who is entrepreneurial, anyone who might claim a larger piece of the pie for himself. (In the Soviet Union, an entrepreneur was a synonym for the word "speculant" and in danger of being sent to a gulag.)

In a growing-pie culture, I can afford to trust others and yield to their interests, sacrificing my own. Why? Because of my belief in a growing pie. It leads me to believe that if I sacrifice my interests now, for the benefit of the other party, it will enable his efforts to make the pie grow and I will eventually receive a larger piece myself.

My point is that trust is not some altruistic and pious notion. It is a form of behavior based on a logical belief system. It is in our self-interest to trust and thus encourage others to work hard and find their reward in a larger piece of the pie because eventually we will receive a bigger piece ourselves.

A matter of self-interest

Let me repeat: It is in our interest to trust.

Here are some musings about how this applies in my analysis of the United States and elsewhere.

American culture has been based until now on mutual trust (and respect). I am constantly amazed that the IRS at least in the past trusted people to report their income honestly for tax purposes. It does not happen in countries of my childhood, and now I know why. There the belief system is based on the concept of a fixed pie and everyone is checking on everyone else.

In the US, the culture has been defined by an attitude that "the sky is the limit," and if you work hard you can make it big. Moreover you will be encouraged to do so.

In a fixed-pie culture the opposite occurs. If you are too entrepreneurial and stand out, people resent you. They put sticks in your wheel, trying to derail you. It was typical of old Europe.

I think the belief in a growing-pie system within the United States emerged out of the vast size of this country and its largely unpopulated regions. There was space and opportunity for everyone. Just work hard.

Today the belief in a growing pie is very much alive in Silicon Valley, in high tech, and on Wall Street, but less so elsewhere in the nation. We read news accounts of the one percent getting richer, while the rest of the country feels their lives are becoming meaner and narrower, and that the pie has become fixed, in fact is shrinking, for everyone else. It is creating strong antagonism against well-to-do entrepreneurs. Thus the Occupy Wall Street behavior. There is increasing animosity against those who have made it.

With a decline in trust internal disintegration begins to set in within the body politic and the society at large. The culture becomes narrower, meaner and the political and economic system itself starts to deteriorate.

Quo vadis America?

How to Treat Corruption[1]

EVERYWHERE, literally in every country I have worked in, people complain about corruption. Mexico, Slovenia, Serbia, Russia, Israel, even the United States. Maybe in Switzerland people do not complain about corruption, but even if that is true, it does not change my observation: A country without corruption is a rare find.

In order to know how to treat corruption, we have to understand its causes, and for that purpose we need to ask ourselves why corruption is universal.

Why? Because change is universal.

The relationship between change and corruption

I suggest to you that one major factor that causes corruption is uncontrolled, unmanageable change; or no change, or very little change in a country which, nevertheless, needs to perform in a changing environment. Why are change and corruption related?

In Hebrew there is an expression: "A hole in the fence invites the thief." All of us, I suggest, have a little larceny in our souls. There are very, very few saints. We should not assume that saints would ever come to populate the whole world. It is simply unrealistic to think the world can be or will be different. If there is a hole in the fence, if we perceive that we can be a little bit corrupt without getting caught, there is a chance we might succumb to the temptation.

There is a similar expression in Serbian: "Those who work with honey cannot help sticking their fingers in the pot to taste it." In other words, we are all human. We differ merely by the degree of resistance we have to temptation.

1. Adizes Insights, July 2012.

I suggest to you that the problem to be addressed is not the "thief" that we all have in us, but the "holes" that tempt us. What, exactly, are those "holes," and what creates them?

How fast do market needs change? In modern society, the changes are very fast and very often. Now, how long does it take to build and implement a system to serve market needs efficiently? It takes a long time.

Since the needs change fast and the system to satisfy those needs changes much slower, there is a good chance that the system will miss responding to client needs promptly, and by the time the system is developed it will no longer serve clients' needs, because they will have changed.

The conclusion: The higher the rate of change, the faster clients' needs will change and thus the higher the probability that the administrative system will be unhealthy. It will not satisfy clients' needs efficiently, i.e., it will be bureaucratic.

I repeat, for emphasis: The higher the rate of change, the more bureaucracy there will be.

The same is true if there is no change in the macro system. The fact that a macro system does not change much does not mean the subsystems that comprise it do not change. So, if a subsystem changes and the macro system it belongs to does not change as well, "holes," as a manifestation of disintegration, will develop.

Enter the expeditor

Take a society where social values have not changed much but technology is changing fast. There will be holes that need filling like how to handle payments, or whether credit deserves being paid interest or not, etc.

To produce results, one needs to overcome the inefficiencies of bureaucracy, to find a way to fill those "holes." That calls for a "thief," someone who knows how to get things done, for a price. Another word for that price is "corruption."

Take an example. In Santa Barbara, where I live, it is a very time-consuming process to get a building permit, which allows you to do construction on your home or your land. The process is bureaucratic.

People have learned to cope by hiring an "expeditor." This is a person who has recently worked in the planning department, which issues those permits, and thus knows the ins and outs of getting a permit. You pay him, and he finds the short cuts. He does not bribe anyone. He simply knows how to overcome the bureaucracy, to quickly move your plans from one desk to the next.

The role of social values

In Santa Barbara, this is not called corruption, but in my opinion it is a *de facto* bribe. If the *system* were efficient, the expeditor would not be necessary. So, to me, the system is corrupt, which gives corrupt people the opportunity to take advantage of the situation. True, it is not as corrupt as in other countries, where documents move from one desk to the next only if the trail is exceedingly well oiled, i.e., lots of money changes lots of hands, but the phenomena is the same.

Wherever there is bureaucracy, an administrative system not oriented to results, corruption will arise to make the system work. What differs among countries is the degree of corruption. That is a function of the social values at play in that country, and how inefficient the administrative system is versus how much pressure there is for it to perform promptly.

> *What differs among countries is the degree of corruption.*

Granted, greed plays a very important role here but the system of values would not be as negatively productive if the administrative system worked well. Take the court system in many countries. Change in social values to sue rather than to settle overloaded the court system to the point that a judgment might take years to be delivered. People need resolution. That creates a "hole," and someone will find a way to bribe the judge to get the judgment out sooner.

Take another example. A society changed from socialism to capitalism, where how much one earns, how much one possesses, is a measurement of one's worth. There was a change in values. But teachers, policemen, medical doctors, and judges get paid as if the country still had the values of socialism: very little. What happens now? Policemen, doctors, judges, and teachers take bribes and get paid well.

What do we need to do? What is the therapy?

Everywhere, and I mean this literally, *everywhere* I have discussed this topic, people attribute corruption to human greed and lack of integrity. In the Adizes Methodology lingo, that would be attributed to column 1, the column in the chain of causality that attributes the problem to culture, values, or leadership style.

I beg to differ. I think corruption belongs to column 6, where we attribute the problems to be a systemic manifestation of systemic processes, systemic structure, and values. The treatment for column 6 is very different from how we treat column 1.

Closing the fence

How different? If we attributed the problem to human greed and lack of integrity the treatment would be to change human nature. Since, I suggest to you, human nature is unchangeable, we should not expect changing human nature to be the solution. So far, no one has succeeded. In fact, not even God could change human nature: The last time He tried, He created the Flood, and after that He was forced to admit it was a lost cause.

Certainly it is possible to *arrest* the problem: catch someone who is blatantly corrupt and execute him. Make him an example for all to see. Scare people. That is what the Chinese are doing. Or put them in jail for many years. That is what the Americans are doing. Arresting or executing corrupt people will halt the problem—for a while.

Corruption does not survive well in full sunlight.

How about educating people to behave honestly? That will also offer some relief.

But do either of these strategies solve the problem? No. I do not need to provide evidence here. Everyone sees it daily in the newspapers. Corruption continues.

To *solve* the problem, we need to close the holes in the fence!

Treating the whole system

Getting back to categorizing the problem, it belongs in column 6. To solve corruption, rather than just *arrest* it, it is necessary to deal with columns 2, 3, 4, and 5. In other words, you have to treat the whole system.

Let us define "treating the whole system." While change is galloping ahead, the cart attached to it is falling apart. The faster the holes develop, the faster we have to close them. We need a full-time maintenance crew working to find and close the holes—but it must do so without stopping the horse. They have to chase the horse and repair the cart on the run.

On a national level, this would be done at the highest level of the government: let's say a deputy prime minister with a significant ministry in terms of budget and people. His staff would be agents of change, professionals whose training is in systems analysis and change management. Their mission is not to find corruption and punish those who are corrupt. That is for the prosecutor general to do. This ministry must be dedicated to finding out how corruption happens, and to reengineering the system so that it is transparent, known to all, and serves clients rapidly and efficiently.

Corruption does not survive well in full sunlight.

The same solution should be repeated at every level of government, down to state and municipal governments, and all large corporations, which are often just as bureaucratic as governments.

Corruption is a question of values, granted. But the solution is not to just change values, which amounts to changing people. We need to fix the system that tempts the weak in soul and spirit. We need to fix the system at least as fast as the system is changing and developing those holes that are the source of the problem.

Is There a Problem with Democracy?[1]

I AM WATCHING THE NEWS and day after day I see demonstrations. Everywhere. In country after country. Some of the demonstrations are violent.

One could say that demonstrations, even violent ones, are an expression of democracy and to suppress them, like Putin is trying to do in Russia, is to suppress democracy.

But theoretically speaking, there should be no demonstrations in a democracy, and for sure no violent ones. Just vote the leaders out of power and put in power those who would lead you in the direction you prefer. In the US the population tried to do that and what happened? Those newly elected leaders very soon were considered "no good" either.

Looking for leadership

One notices that there is a seesaw phenomena. If, for instance, the X party is in power, people vote for the Y party which was in opposition and when the Y party is in power, they vote for the X again. Watch the elections in England. People vote for the Left, then in the next elections for the Right, and then back to Left.

People are desperately looking for leadership to lead them in the direction they trust to be the right one. Since those in power, whoever they are, are considered to be not trustworthy, people look for a replacement, only to find out that the new ones are not that different. At a certain point, people lose respect and trust for both parties, as happened in Greece, and then who gets elected? Someone who was not in power and thus has not been tested yet, and thus has not been criticized yet either. See Italy or the winning party in Greece. People will elect someone who had no experience ruling or leading, and because of that has no record. Another example? Barack Obama.

---

1. Adizes Insights, September 2012.

People are getting disenchanted with the election process as a vehicle to be ruled the way they want to be ruled. Instead of voting the prescribed way, which they apparently do not trust to work anymore, they vote with their feet: Demonstrate. Burn tires. Smash windows. Fight the police who represent those in power.

People are desperately looking for leadership. I acknowledge that demonstrations can be useful to express voters' desires and force the government to react. Take, for example, the civil rights movement. Another example of a demonstration that worked is the opposition to the war in Vietnam.

But demonstrations are emotionally expensive. They cost lives: Dr. King, four students at Kent State University, and civil rights workers in Mississippi are examples.

Democracy then and now

Is that what we want? Do we need to demonstrate, burn tires, and smash windows to make our desires known and addressed?

Democracy worked in small systems. Athens. The New England city hall. In systems where people knew each other, where the elected leaders were in touch with their voters, and where the complexity of the problems was not acute. Today, we live in a very complex environment. Problems are systemic in nature and whoever is the leader, and whichever party he or she represents, cannot solve these problems without getting criticized endlessly or demonstrated against.

The democratic system was created generations ago when the world was simpler. When the pace of life was slower. When people did not have the "I deserve to be taken care of" expectation. Where the mode of behavior was one of giving rather than one of taking. A world of self-reliance, not of dependency.

In the new world of entitlement we live in—of "give us bread and entertainment or we will burn the house down," a world where people do not want to sacrifice, where they would rather be instantly gratified—being a leader of a democratic system, which depends on those people, with the values and behavior described above, to be reelected, it is a call for being endlessly humiliated and criticized.

Who wants to be a leader in this situation? What kind of people do we elect?

We need to re-engineer the democratic system if it is going to attract the leadership we want, if it is going to stop violence as a means of expression.

SHOULD GOVERNMENTS SUE FOR DEFAMATION?[1]

I JUST READ IN THE *Moscow Times*, a local English daily, that the Orange County, California Water District Board is suing someone for defamation. This someone, a private citizen, has sent emails claiming corruption by the Board in allocating water rights. The article goes on to say that lawyers, who apparently specialize in this field of the law, claim that the Board cannot win this case. As a matter of fact, the Board should not have even sued because, according to the law, government cannot sue citizens for defamation.

The reason such a law exists, the article claims, is that if the deep-pocketed government could sue whistle blowers, who do not have the same resources to defend themselves, it would discourage anyone from criticizing the government and corruption would flourish. The government would suppress opposition and hold on to power even though they do not deserve it.

Why was this article published in Russia? Because a law is being passed through their parliament that will levy prohibitively heavy fines (almost a year's average take-home income) on any demonstrator who demonstrates without a permit.

I believe this article was a subtle way to criticize the Russian government for suppression.

Art imitates life, life imitates art

But is there a reason why governments can and should sue individuals?

It has become fashionable to badmouth government and politicians. It is not just in fictional stories, in movies and books that depict politicians as corrupt to the core. It is in editorials, in letters to the editors. It is everywhere.

Some accusations might be true. And some are pure fiction, serving someone's interests to undermine those in power.

1. Adizes Insights, September 2012.

But, the end result is that these accusations feed a frenzy of hatred toward politicians. It is not only art that imitates life; life imitates art too.

As the attacks intensify, they have a cumulative effect that impacts the degree of trust followers have in their leaders, and people will reject their leaders even when the reasons for rejection are questionable.

To me, management of a company, parenting a family, and governing a country have a common denominator: Their role is to provide the healthy envelope within which we strive to succeed in life. To be able to perform that task, parents need to be trusted. The same applies to management of companies, and this is not less true for politicians. They all perform a role of leadership, and leadership does not perform well without the trust of followers.

Would you allow your children to badmouth the mother of the family, for instance? Or, as a manager, would you pass over, without reaction, being defamed by a subordinate? Why are politicians different?

A wrong solution

The argument given above is that if the government sues, with its vast financial resources, with brigades of lawyers on its payroll, the government will squash, bulldoze its citizens into submission. No one will dare to criticize politicians or the government, and corruption will have free rein.

This is the wrong conclusion, I say. The solution is not to forbid the government from suing. The solution is to legislate that whistleblowers have the right to protection paid for by the government.

I remember the first time I came across this question of how politicians get defamed. The Adizes International Convention that we hold annually was, that time, in Eilat, a resort city on the shores of the Red Sea, Israel. At the head table sitting next to me was the mayor of the city. He asked me what Adizes was. I started to tell him about mutual trust and respect, which is what we bring to companies to minimize internal conflicts that are destructive and create a culture of constructive, collaborative relations. As I was talking, I became aware that his face was showing disbelief, and by curling his lips, he was communicating to me: "Come on, be real. Are you naïve or what? Grow up!"

So, I asked him what he thinks about what I just told him.

"It will not work in politics, in government," he said. "When my opponent goes all over town telling everyone that my sister is a whore, how easy is it for me to tell the people that I do not even have a sister? Bad news travels fast, easy. It spreads like fire. Good news move at the speed of mud."

Bad news travels fast, easy. It spreads like fire. Good news move at the speed of mud.

I became quiet. I realized that he was right. Working with eight prime ministers from eight different countries, I noticed how thick-skinned they have to be to lead a country. I noticed that anyone who is even a bit sensitive will not run for office if his life depends on it. He would be putting his reputation on line, endangering his family relations, and subjecting himself to continuous humiliation.

The game of politics

Politics is the dirtiest war there is. To win power politicians throw not mud but fecal matter at each other all day long. They lie about each other, spin information, and twist the truth. The result is that the population does not trust any of them. The country becomes functionally leaderless. It is like parents who bad mouth each other in front of their children, and not just by calling each other bad names, but by accusing each other of atrocious things. What do children of such parents do in such situations? They run away from home, become homeless, become drug addicts and child prostitutes....

What do citizens of countries where all trust of politicians has evaporated do? They leave the country if they can, and if they cannot, they burn tires, smash windows, battle the police, and feel hopeless. Or they join the corruption wagon if they can.

We must protect the good name of our leaders and those who govern us without giving them the right to suppress us.

How? Government should be able to use taxpayers' money to sue taxpayers, and the same source of money should be available to taxpayers to defend themselves from the government. We should allow governments to sue. And government should finance the defense of whoever accuses the government. Whoever loses, however, pays the damages.

THE BENEFITS OF DIVERSITY[1]

THERE IS A SAYING that the most beautiful girls in the Soviet Union were in Ukraine and the most beautiful ones in Ukraine were in Odessa. Assuming that is true, why Odessa? And why does Israel have very beautiful people? And Belgrade as well? Sweden has beautiful people too, but—and here is the insight—in Sweden they all look the same. Not true for Odessa. Or Belgrade, or Israel. There they are exotic looking, each one different and more beautiful than the other.

What is the difference, and what is the common denominator?

Diversity.

Odessa is located geographically in a place where multiple cultures and ethnic groups passed through or settled. As a result there was considerable intermarriage and exotic, beautiful people emerged. The same is true for Belgrade, which is where Turkish influence (five hundred years of occupation) and European culture met. Israel is another petri dish of diversity, where the Jews from seventy countries migrated. You have black immigrants from Ethiopia intermarrying with immigrants from Europe.

Diversity creates beauty. Sameness is boring.

Diversity creates beauty. Sameness is boring.

Think of a jungle and compare it to a desert. Which is more alive? Beautiful? Exciting? Now imagine a jungle penetrated by a foreign aggressive weed that destroys all indigenous flora. Eventually diversity is destroyed and a lifeless environment dominates the scene.

1. Adizes Insights, May 2013.

Are radical Islam and other extremist movements the foreign weed that is threatening our diversity?

Without diversity there is no ecology. And without functioning ecology there is no life. Aggressive weeds need to be pulled out so that diversified flora can flourish. We do this when we garden. Does it apply to managing our country?

THE COLLATERAL DAMAGES OF MULTINATIONALS[1]

I HAVE BEEN CONSULTING to major corporations and family-run businesses for over forty years. My analysis here, in this blog, is not based on "scientific" research. I have not built in a representative sample. I did not conduct interviews, nor was there an extensive search of the literature on the subject. These are pure observations on my part based on many years of involvement with actual corporate decision making. My conclusions, due to the limited sample, might be wrong, and I would appreciate feedback.

Sustainability

Sustainability is a very hot subject. We are all worried about the environment and are conscious that we have to protect this "little ball of life" floating in space. So, we need to stop water, air, and land pollution. And stop polluting people's health by feeding them food that makes them obese and diabetic, and, in general, runs down their health.

> *I find that local companies care about their reputation.*

Who is more prone to pollute? Will a CEO pollute the air in the community in which he or she lives? Not likely. He or she would be socially ostracized. It is natural to care about affiliation and how one is regarded by neighbors and friends. Not to mention that a CEO will rarely make decisions that threaten the health of his family which lives in that community.

But what if the plant is thousands of miles away? In a foreign country? In a community in which he knows no one personally? Well, then, he might just allow pollution, especially if that decision increases earnings per share and, of course, increases his net worth.

1. Adizes Insights, October 2013.

I find that local companies care about their reputation. Their clients are the neighbors. The name of the founder is often on the letterhead. They usually are concerned about what they do and how it is accepted by the community.

Not so for multinationals. Here the story is different. It appears to me that for them "sustainability" is a percentage of their expense budget. It is more of a PR effort.

I just returned from Bled, Slovenia, where I attended a conference on responsible management, (PRME) an offshoot of the Global Compact of the United Nations. Under the terms set by the Global Compact, companies sign a pact to be socially responsible. At the conference I met an endowed-chair professor: The Coca-Cola Professor on Sustainability. I could not resist wondering: Is this not the same Coca-Cola that provides sugar-loaded drinks, which cause obesity and lead to diabetes? And is it not the same Coca-Cola whose Diet Coke is full of questionable chemicals that make it sweet? And they are the one to be professing sustainability?

Give me a break.

How about McDonalds? On one hand it is deeply involved in philanthropy, while, on the other hand, the company turns out hamburger meat for millions that is loaded with chemicals to fatten the cows more quickly. The resultant beef is then cooked with lots of oil and salt, all of which helps to produce worldwide obesity.

Who is kidding whom?

I bet McDonalds' CEO does not feed his family Big Macs. He knows better. But feeding people in the inner city, people he will never meet, that does not cause him to lose much sleep.

I believe it is alienation that causes irresponsible managerial behavior: physical, social, emotional—you name it—alienation, the distance between the decision-maker and the consumers. The multinational corporations exhibit it the most because they are large and spread around the globe.

Centralization

In my consulting, I often come across companies that are branches of a multinational company. The locals would like to democratize the local company, make it more participative, empower people, etc. But their authority to make decisions is limited. Very limited. There is a VP thousands of miles away who decides how the local company will run. The local management is constrained, disempowered. Its leaders cannot make any decisions that involve change.

There are repercussions. Those constraints over time impact how people feel empowered in general. The entrepreneurial spirit is more limited when you are led rather than when you lead. I suggest that this impacts democracy. If people cannot make decisions about their working environment why would they feel empowered to influence decisions made by their politicians?

Taxes

Large corporations like Apple and General Electric have been in the news lately for legally avoided paying billions in taxes by moving revenues and expenses between their foreign entities to countries with lower taxes.

How does a businessman who is not running a multinational feel when hit with increasing taxation? How does a small-business owner who is struggling to make a go of his company, one who carries a significant and increasing burden of taxes, feel when he reads how giants like Apple or GE legally paid very little or no taxes? Does he believe it is fair?

Does it not broaden alienation between people and their government? What does it do to trust and respect? Does not alienation destroy it?

Financial Resources

The big companies have an advantage when it comes to securing finances. They have more to show; more resources and sophistication to support their requests. I find that banks are not that interested in the small and even medium-sized companies. Frequently the small and medium-sized companies have a hell of a time finding financial resources.

Resources are finite and the more that goes to the big fish the less there is for the small ones.

This is not insignificant. Why? Because democracy needs a middle class. It needs entrepreneurs. Unless you are a high-tech start-up attracting private equity funds, or a large company with a great balance sheet, you will have trouble resourcing finances. And so, not surprisingly, the middle class is shrinking.

Small is beautiful. Not as efficient, granted—there are economies of scale in size. But what we gain economically we lose politically, socially, and physically.

How Change Causes Corruption[1]

ORRUPTION IS A PROBLEM for most countries; they engage in a constant struggle to overcome it, often with little success. I know of few nations that are immune to the disease; maybe Singapore or Switzerland. I am unsure. But in my travels around the world, working in different countries, I encounter the same complaint: *"Corruption."*

What are the causes of corruption? Why is it so widespread? Is it just an inborn trait in which people everywhere have corrupt value systems? Or is there more to it than that?

> *I believe corruption is a more complex phenomenon than simply a failure of human values.*

I believe corruption is a more complex phenomenon than simply a failure of human values. Its roots are found elsewhere within our social system(s). Ultimately, it has to do not just with human frailty, but with *change*.

Take any device and expose it to drastic, severe change and what will happen? Pull it. Pull it some more from different directions...and what are the results? It will come apart.

It is the same with systems. They develop gaps, cracks, and fissures when subject to change. During the course of repeated change, the system finally breaks down.

If we look at a nation that was once a colony, we might observe a series of multiple laws. Some date from colonial times; some are new. And, some are very, very recent and overlap with both the colonial and the so-called, "new laws." Often, the end result is major confusion as to what is right and what is wrong. We see this today in many African nations.

1. Adizes Insights, May 2014.

A similar pattern (of confusion) occurs in nations that have had quite different political and/or economic systems over the course of their history.

Which brings us to Russia. Ruled by a tsar and a bureaucracy; followed by a violent revolution and a supreme (Communist) political system with its accompanying bureaucracy; followed in turn by a relatively peaceful revolution and a new market economy system (not very free, but still....) departing from a central planning system, and what you get is a lot of change.

Today, Russia has three different accounting systems, all legitimate. Imagine what that can do to comparative financial results. Imagine how it impacts auditing efforts. And, now imagine in this situation how difficult or relatively easy is it to cheat or steal...

Moreover, as change accelerates anywhere in the world, collateral problems arise like pollution, urban overcrowding, and transportation problems; or how to control sanitation, or regulate the quality of food production and distribution.

A call for controls

All of this calls for regulation. For controls. For *systems* of control. For permits and licenses.

Often, the systems do not change fast enough to keep up with what needs to be controlled; change outpaces the capability of people and governments to adapt to the new conditions; to develop new or improved systems. There is a constant sense of falling behind.

The result is called a bureaucracy. It can block the capability of companies to act in a changing environment that requires prompt action.

So, we have two problems caused by change for most nations (among many which are not necessarily related to this article); gaps develop (i.e., people have no clear idea what needs to be done, when it needs to be done or how to do it), and bureaucratization of the systems settles in place. The system works all right, but at a pace that is awfully slow and inefficient. Meanwhile, the needs of the market responding to change have revved up and demand a prompt response.

This is where corruption comes to play a role. A client who needs to make the system work has to find ways to speed up the bureaucratization process; make it shorter and more efficient. How to do that seems fairly clear. Find someone who knows the ropes, who will make the system work (rapidly).

And, since such a service has value for that client, he or she will be willing to pay for it. When you pay—place your money on or under the table—you have contributed to the phenomenon called "corruption."

Take a buyer in a retail chain or someone who is in charge of buying for a government institution. Here is where one is prone to find corruption. The suppliers try to pay a "fee" so that they can be moved to the head of the line; so that they can suddenly be the preferred supplier. A great deal of money is at stake.

The more change in the country, the more bureaucracy.

The buyer in this scenario is placed in a position where he can abuse his power. He has to decide who will get the contract. In effect he chooses from whom to buy. And that decision can be influenced by who pays the most under the table.

Now, see where the problem is: It resides in the company or government agency where bribes occur. I suggest to you, it does not have a transparent system or a working audit system of purchasing practices. If it did, it would have prohibited this "under the table" transaction from happening.

It does not have a well-functioning system because much has changed over time, making the system opaque, not transparent or broken down.

The opaqueness means lack of controls in the company which has created the conditions that can be exploited by some of its staff.

I suggest to you that the better the systems are able to function, the more transparent they are, and the more controllable. One result: there will be less corruption.

Here is the formula:

> The more change in the country, the more bureaucracy.
>
> The more bureaucracy within a changing environment, the more corruption.

Punishing the corrupt people does not solve the problem. It might slow it down, even arrest it. However, the problem of corruption will not be ended.

It is like killing mosquitoes that carry malaria. You cannot kill them all. And, if you kill some, new ones are born. You need to dry the swamps where they breed.

We cannot punish, let alone execute all those who are corrupt. Nor can we slow down the change that is creating the "gaps" or the bureaucratization.

But, we can accelerate how we de-bureaucratize the system, and re-engineer it, so there are no longer ongoing "holes." And continuously re-engineer the system to successfully and promptly serve the clients who depend on the system to fulfill their market needs.

For a country experiencing chronic change, I would like to see a ministry in charge of de-bureaucratization, re-systematization. A model already exists within corporations that have systems engineering or continuous improvement departments. (This is what the Adizes Institute is dedicated to doing on both a corporate and a governmental level worldwide). It can be done. And should be done.

What is needed is less prosecution, more prevention.

PART VI

❋

SOCIAL CHALLENGES

Why I Say No to Tolerance[1]

IT IS IN VOGUE to promote the idea of tolerance among ethnic groups, races and religions. In Santa Barbara, where I live, there is a whole program in schools providing educational material about tolerance. In Washington, D.C., the museum about the atrocities of the Holocaust is called the Museum of Tolerance.

What is wrong?

Seeking the positive

Assume you and your wife fight a lot. The prescription someone gives you both is that you should "tolerate" each other. Tolerate? It means, to me, to yield to an impulse to express your preference and become passive instead; to surrender to the reality that you cannot stand differences. To me, to tolerate others who are different sounds like to suffer quietly.

So what is the alternative? To fight? To kill each other? To reject the differences?

> *My prescription is to rejoice in the differences.*

No! My prescription is to rejoice in the differences. To actively seek the positive that the difference offers. When a man introduces his spouse should he say, "This is my wife whom I quietly tolerate," or should he introduce her as his "better half?"

Being different means that the other party, by definition, has something different to offer. Why not actively search for that enriching difference rather than just tolerate the uncomfortable difference?

The Gypsies can be tolerated or we can rejoice in their music, their love for living in the moment.

1. Adizes Insights, April 2011.

The Jewish people can be tolerated for their idiosyncrasies, like being highly passionate about whatever their particular belief is (sometimes interpreted as being "pushy"), or we can appreciate their dedication to education, their relentless search for knowledge, the sharpness of their mind.

Every person, every nation, culture, sexual orientation...every flower or weed has a story to tell. Do not just tolerate it. Learn the story. Embrace the learning and rejoice the difference offered.

WHAT DOES "ONE" MEAN?[1]

A S I WAS WALKING TODAY I passed a church. It had a big sign in front inviting anyone to come in and be "one." It made me think. This is what we all want to be: *one.* To be integrated as a family, as a community, and even as a person; to stop the struggle with those who disagree with us and to stop the debate we often have between our ears.

> *We need to believe that we can be one and not necessarily the same.*

But what does it mean to be *one*? I believe that for many it means that there are no more differences. That is what drove the inquisitors behind the Inquisition. That is what is driving the behavior of many fanatic religious people, not only the radical Muslims. That is what drove Communism and fascism, too: no more diversity. Be like me or be damned. Oneness is a lofty goal, but the means of achieving this goal have been tragic. How many people died or suffered because some regimes, religions, or political movements were trying by all means to achieve this most desirable goal of oneness?

Reframing the concept

It occurs to me that we might want to reframe what we understand under the word or concept of *one.* Look at your hand. Different size fingers working in unison as a hand. We need to believe that we can be *one* and not necessarily the *same.* That there can be unity in diversity.

How? For unity in diversity there must be a common denominator that unites the diverse components without undermining their uniqueness, their differences. What is that common denominator?

1. Adizes Insights, December 2011.

I believe it is mutual trust and respect. Mutual trust, meaning that people believe that they are in a symbiotic relationship, where each participant in the interaction will benefit from contributing differently. Each contributes that in which they have a competitive advantage, and each benefits from what the other has to offer. (For those of you for whom the concept of competitive advantage is foreign, I suggest reading Paul Samuelson's book *Introduction to Economics.* In it he gives an example of one country that is skilled in growing oranges and another that is better at producing cars; by exchanging oranges for cars, both countries benefit. What holds for countries holds for people, too.) If there is mutual trust, differences enrich, rather than endanger, one's position.

Mutual respect means that the diverse components are open to learning from those who are different from them. Again, with mutual respect people benefit from diversity rather than being stymied by it.

In economic terms, mutual respect means open markets—no barriers to trade. Mutual trust means one does not exploit open trade to benefit itself at the expense of the other. In interpersonal relations it means not just tolerance of diversity but nourishment of constructive diversity. We appreciate what diversity contributes to the system and to each one of us.

Benefits of diversity

Diversity based on MT&R enriches all those involved. They learn from each other's differences and thus know more than they would have known cumulatively but without interaction, and they benefit from the increased wealth they have created together. Without MT&R, diversity causes disintegration, a breakdown of the system.

What holds us back from reframing our thinking that oneness should not mean sameness—that it is integration, not fusion—is fear. Fear of the unknown, of differences we do not know how to control. Sameness, the usual interpretation of oneness, gives us a sense of being in control: The components of the system are known and their behavior predictable. But that brings bureaucracy, and eliminates creativity and innovation, thus reducing economic growth and well-being.

What is most controllable is not necessarily what is the most desirable.

An Aging Population: Problems[1]

YEARS AGO—some of us still remember—children were an investment. At that time, there was no health insurance, life insurance, or pension plans. Parents invested in their children and expected their children to take care of them if they got sick and when they got old. Children were not regarded as an investment only for the long run. They were expected to be productive and add value to the family even while they were still growing. Girls helped with housework; boys worked in the field.

I, for example, started working at the age of 11, when my father was hurt in a work-related accident. For a while, I was actually responsible for supporting my family. When my father got cancer at age 55, he stopped working altogether, and I supported my parents for the next thirty years until they both passed away. They had no life insurance, no pension plans. I took complete responsibility for my parents' well-being.

All that has changed, at least in developed countries. People have insurance and pension plans. They put funds away during their working lives to pay for an old-age home, or assisted-living facility, where they will be taken care of by paid caregivers. They even insure the cost of their own burial; God forbid their children should have to carry that burden.

While children are no longer an asset, the liability of having them has increased many folds. For one, the price of children's education has gone sky high, but that is the "easy" cost to bear. What about the emotional and psychological costs to keep the children away from drugs, which are all over the place, in every school; the efforts to impress upon them the dangers of unprotected sex and of unplanned pregnancies; and the time and effort to protect them from numerous other very powerful negative influences?

---

1. Adizes Insights, May 2012.

They are a high-priced investment, with little or no return. I am not just referring to monetary returns. Children used to give their parents and grandparents respect, which was the most valuable and satisfying return. But, this rarely happens anymore.

Respect: An illustration

Let me share some experiences to illustrate what respect feels like in a Jewish religious family. It is Friday evening and time to welcome the Sabbath. Everyone must be home early and be ready for the prayers before the first star appears in the sky. The family gathers for the Friday evening meal. No one is late. The whole family dresses festively, the men often in white shirts, and everyone sits around the table, with the father at the head of the table.

First, the family washes their hands. From that moment on until the blessing is read, there is absolute silence and throughout the meal, the children are obedient and, if old enough, help serve the meal. The table is set with food. The mother is beaming with pride. The food on the table, the family around the table: This is her portfolio of success in her role of making a house into a home.

Now, the father sings a song, which is a chapter from the Old Testament, about a valiant woman. He is praising the woman of the house, who earns the family's respect for being a valiant wife and mother. Next, the father gets up, kisses his wife on the cheek, and goes to each of his children, one at a time. Each child, of any age, kisses the father's hand, and the father blesses the child, while putting that hand on the top of the child's head.

Next, the wine is blessed, and a single wine glass especially dedicated to the blessing of the wine is filled and passed around the table to be shared, from one family member to another, until each person has had a sip.

Then comes the blessing of the bread: The father takes the challah, the braided bread that is baked especially for the Sabbath, and gives a piece of it to every member of the family—first the mother, then the eldest child, etc. This symbolizes that he is the bread earner, and the one who feeds the family. It is recognized respectfully and thankfully by the family. The bread is shared and blessed.

Now is the time for everyone, including the children, to sing traditional Sabbath songs while the food is served. At the end of the meal, a blessing is sung to thank the Lord for providing food for the family and keeping them healthy.

This is the ritual in which, in one way or another, the family expresses respect, appreciation, and love to each other and especially to the parents.

Now compare this to the modern world in which we live. If you have a TV at home, eventually you will probably barely recognize your children. They will have a language of their own, which they have picked up from TV programs or computer games you do not watch or play. They will wear their hair in styles that, had I tried when I was a teenager, I would have been kicked out of the house in no time. They will have piercings in their ears, lips, tongue, nose, and even eyelids, and tattoos anywhere and everywhere.

There is no economic return in having children anymore.

Who are those kids? Where did they come from? They look like aliens.

They learn disrespect for authority, to talk back, to interrupt their elders. The kids take phone calls during the meal, or text each other under the table, or leave the table altogether to talk to their friends, without even asking if it is okay.

There is no economic return in having children anymore. And the unfortunate truth is that there is no psychological return, either. (I just read somewhere why today's children are called the Y generation: "Y should I work? Y should I clean my room? Y do you not let me do whatever I want…?")

Now, whose fault is this? There are no bad soldiers, just bad generals. There are no bad workers, just incompetent managers. And, by the same token, there are no bad kids, just neglectful parents.

I feel that modern society has abandoned its most important role, and that is to secure the quality of the next generation. We are not only destroying the environment for the next generations and leaving a staggering debt for them to carry, we are also doing a lousy job of raising them.

I am not referring only to formal education. I am referring to their attitude, their behavior.

Respect for parents is one of the Ten Commandments. Think of it, why is it so important? When respect is lost, the family fabric that ties us together is torn apart and the basic cell of society is destroyed.

As children become more of a liability than an asset, parents cut down on the number of children they have. The result is an aging population. Countries where the population is aging are going to have serious demographic problems, problems that will affect their economies, traditions, and social structure. We need to start thinking about what it will take to turn the tide, to improve our dedication to parenting. And no time is soon enough.

The Scarcity of
Smiling People[1]

I THINK I DID A DISSERVICE to the Russian people in my recent blog post where I said that I cannot find smiling people on the streets of Moscow. What I said is still true, but my conclusions were wrong. I do not see smiling faces in New York, or London, or any large city for that matter. If you want to see a smiling person, go to a very small hamlet, to a village where life moves slowly. I bet that if I went to a small Russian city I would find people smiling at me on the street.

I remember coming from New York, where I studied at Columbia, to Los Angeles in 1967. What pleasantly surprised me was how people on the street smiled at me. I was not used to that in New York. But that is history. No one smiles in Los Angeles anymore. It grew too big. The rush hour is not an hour long anymore. It is a rush day and night. To see people smile, come to small Santa Barbara, but hurry up because it is growing too.

I think that there is a correlation between the size of the population of a city and whether the people in that city smile or not. The more populous the city, the more crowded the roads, the more hurried the people seem to be, and the more scorning faces, and fewer smiling faces, one will encounter.

So it is not just Moscow.

A struggle to survive

Years ago I read an article which described an experiment conducted with rats. They put rats in a box. As long as there were few of them, they acted normally. When the box became overcrowded, however, their behavior changed drastically. The rate of sexual activity increased, including the rate of homosexual intercourse. Furthermore, they started killing each other.

1. Adizes Insights, June 2012.

The common denominator to such behavior—the increase in sexual behavior and the fatal attacks on each other—is, I believe, the struggle for survival. On one hand, the rats try to diminish their numbers by killing each other and, at the same time, fearing extinction they increase copulation.

Is that what is happening with humans in large cities?

> *There is a correlation between the size of the population of a city and whether the people in that city smile or not.*

As population increases, let us say, measured by people per square mile, crime rate increases, aggression increases, smiles disappear, community singing is a relic of the past, and loneliness and depression are common. Taking a cue from the rats, as the planet is becoming more and more populated, should we conclude that a nuclear holocaust is inevitable? It will be one way by which population will be regulated. Will incurable diseases that are resistant to any drugs proliferate?

If the twentieth century was the bloodiest century of human civilization, as people murdered other people more than in any other century, is it just a preamble to what will happen on a much larger scale in the twenty-first century? Is there an exit from this predicament?

Here is a thought. As the numbers of people increase, the value of any one individual decreases. This is Economic Theory 101: When there is "inflation" of people, their value decreases. When people are scarce, their value increases.

I remember going on a walking safari with my two sons in 1991 in Botswana, on the border of Namibia. We walked and canoed with a guide without seeing another human being for a week. When eventually we came across one, we treated him like we would treat a long-lost close relative or a best friend we had not seen for a long time.

We need to educate people about the value of human life. We need to value life more than ever before. Art and the humanities should play a major role more than ever before.

As our numbers increase we need to consciously work on overcoming our subconscious tendency to destroy ourselves.

GETTING OLDER YOUNGER[1]

ONE OF THE RESULTS of the rapid change we are experiencing in modern times is that people are getting older younger.

Let me explain. Today, if someone is 40 years old in the high-tech industry and searching for work, he will probably find it difficult to find employment. No one will tell him why, because it is against the law to discriminate on the basis of age, but the reason is clear: He is too old.

My God! Too old at 40.

> ## My God! Too old at 40.

If your professional experience has been connected to the internet or to a web-based field and you are suddenly unemployed, you will find that 40 is not old, but ancient. Employers are on the lookout for more recent graduates, men and women in their twenties, those with the latest, cutting-edge education.

My son is a musician. At the age of 19, he left college because, he claims, in new-age and electronic music (which he writes) if he does not make it by 23, he will have been passed by. Almost obsolete. No chance of making it at all. Too old.

The reason is obvious: change. Social taste in fashion and music is changing very rapidly. And the new technology—blink and you miss some major development—is driving the change. You must be capable of learning continuously, and learning fast at that. Unfortunately, this ability to learn quickly diminishes with age, and employers do not want to cope with it; they do not want the burden of retraining someone. This is my understanding.

In the past, a generation was considered to be thirty-three years long. Today, I suggest to you it is no more than ten years, if not less.

1. Adizes Insights, January 2014.

I have six kids. They are 38, 37, 36, 30, 29, and 19. My immediate family consists of five different generations. That's how many congregate at home over holidays and for birthdays. I (at 76) am one. My wife is a different generation; she is twenty years younger. The three oldest children are the third generation. The 30- and 29-year-old are the fourth, and the "baby," at 19, is the fifth generation.

How do I know? We have five different value systems. Different expectations from life. Different lifestyles. It is as though we speak five different languages. I am not the only one who says this. The children say that about each other.

This phenomenon, that we are getting older younger, has many repercussions.

Older but not smarter

Alas, just because one is older does not necessarily mean that he is smarter or even more knowledgeable. I feel like an idiot when confronted with new electronic devices I can barely handle. I turn sheepishly (or in frustration) to my teenage son who has to explain to me what to do and how to do it. In the process, I feel my authority as a parent slipping away from me. Instead of father teaching son, it is now the reverse: son teaching parent. Authority gets shaken, if not undermined, and the hierarchy within the family is fractured.

Nor is it necessarily easier on the younger generation. Today, the pressure on young professionals to make it early or be left behind is much heavier than when I was young.

Major changes that used to take thirty years to unfold and be recognized now take ten. What does this bode for the future? Every five years a new generation? Three years? Being considered too old and "over the hill" at 23… not just in music, but in fashion, science, and who knows what else? What is the future? Teenagers running the world? They might know the technology and the latest fads, but emotionally they are not grown up yet.

What we are seeing and experiencing is an imbalance between emotional maturation and career development.

In my analysis of this phenomenon, this rollercoaster change is detrimental to us as a society. But it cannot be stopped. We need to find ways to accentuate the spiritual and emotional development of our children sooner and faster.

Or else.

About the Adizes Institute

For the past forty years, the Adizes Institute has been committed to equipping visionary leaders, management teams, and agents of change to become champions of their industries and markets. These leaders have successfully established a collaborative organizational culture by using Adizes' pragmatic tools and concepts to achieve peak performance.

Adizes specializes in guiding leaders of organizations (CEOs, top management teams, boards, owners) to quickly and effectively resolve such issues as:

- Difficulties in executing good decisions.
- Making the transition from entrepreneurship to professional management.
- Difficulties in aligning the structure of the organization to achieve its strategic intent.
- "Bureaucratizing": The organization is getting out of touch with its markets and beginning to lose entrepreneurial vitality.
- Conflicts among founders, owners, board members, partners, and family members.
- Internal management team conflicts and "politics" severe enough to inhibit the success of the business.
- Growing pains.
- Culture clashes between companies undergoing mergers or acquisitions.

Adizes also offers comprehensive training and certification for change leaders who wish to incorporate into their practice the Adizes Methodologies for managing change.

Adizes is the primary sponsor of the Adizes Graduate School, a non-profit teaching organization that offers Master's and Ph.D. programs for the Study of Leadership and Change.

For more information about these and other programs, please visit www.adizes.com.